THE SECRET
OF THE SCIENCE OF
GETTING
RICH

T0272969

THE SECRET
OF THE SCIENCE OF
GETTING
RICH

Change Your Beliefs about
Success and Money to
Create the Life You Want

BOB PROCTOR AND
SANDY GALLAGHER

Published 2022 by Gildan Media LLC
aka G&D Media
www.GandDmedia.com

Front Cover design by Patti Knoles

Interior design by Meghan Day Healey of Story Horse, LLC

Library of Congress Cataloging-in-Publication Data is available upon request

ISBN: 978-1-7225-0576-9

10   9   8   7   6   5   4   3   2   1

Contents

Foreword
by Sandy Gallagher

As the title of this book implies, the science of getting rich is not a haphazard bunch of information. It's a methodical, scientific, well-thought-out plan for creating wealth in all aspects of your life.

With everything that's going on right now, we really want to understand what differentiates good and bad. Actually, it's your thinking that determines if something is good or bad. We have a choice: we can choose to focus on what's good, or we can choose to focus on what's not good.

W. Clement Stone, who built the Combined Insurance Company of America, among other accomplishments, developed a philosophy of saying, "That's good," no matter what someone told him. Someone could come up and say, "Your building just burned down," and he would reply, "That's good."

Why would you do that? Because if you say, "That's good" about anything, you're going to find the good in it. It's a beautiful lesson.

The book that got Bob Proctor started in the success industry was Napoleon Hill's classic *Think and Grow Rich*. It says, "Begin to think abundance. A disciplined mind can create a substantial income, starting today."

Bob stopped thinking about bills or debts. He started thinking about abundance, and he set goals for accumulating wealth. That shift made all the difference. When he committed to studying and following the directions of his mentor, his income changed dramatically. He was earning $4,000 a year when he started studying this material, and in one year, his income went to over $175,000.

If you study this material and you exercise discipline in studying, thinking, and acting, you can turn your annual income into your monthly income. Bob, of course, went way beyond that.

One of Bob's most admirable traits was his discipline. Discipline is the ability to give yourself a command and then follow it. You want to begin to think abundance, and you want to exercise discipline in your study of these ideas. The more discipline you exercise, the more you're going to get out of this book. It's all about abundance. It's about prosperity. It's about fulfillment in life.

"Discipline is the ability to give yourself a command, and then follow it."

Lloyd Conant and Earl Nightingale started the industry of audio success recordings. In 1968, when Bob was struggling to get a green card and establish himself in the United States, Lloyd Conant invited him to dinner.

Bob asked, "Lloyd, how did you start this business?"

Lloyd said, "I started this business because of this book." It was *The Science of Getting Rich*, written by Wallace D. Wattles and published in 1910. When Lloyd Conant got his hands on that book, he ate it up. He read the whole thing in one night and kept going back and reading and rereading it.

When Bob heard that, he was fascinated. He said, "I've got to get my hands on this book." Lloyd gave him his own copy, and Bob never put it down. He studied it ever after; he never stopped.

Wattles' book also inspired Rhonda Byrne to create her inspirational movie *The Secret*, which came out in 2006. She knew how Bob had studied this book, so she had him appear in the movie.

That year, this book also changed my life, because it was on August 18, 2006, that I attended my first Bob

Proctor seminar in Vancouver, Washington, and I will never forget it.

At the time, I was an attorney with a corporate securities practice. Basically, I was merging and forming banks and helping them do IPOs and other securities work. I was doing quite well. I was an equity partner in the firm, and I was earning an income in the high six figures. Things seemed pretty good in my life.

When Bob walked out on stage and started talking, he got my attention immediately. I was fascinated with what he was saying. It was as if he took my head off, shook it around, and stuck it back on. I reevaluated everything in my life. A bright light went on, and my world expanded in that moment.

After that three days at Bob's Science of Getting Rich seminar, my world was completely changed. He kept asking, "What do you really want? Don't think about what somebody else wants for you. Don't think about what you think is possible for you. Dig into your heart. If anything were possible, what do you want? How do you want to live your life? What do you want to accomplish?"

My copy of *The Science of Getting Rich* was a little hardbound green book. I opened it up and wrote, "I want to be in the inner circle of this company. I want to be Bob Proctor's closest advisor. I want to create a program with him to bring into companies and boardrooms and executive offices." I wrote this in tiny print, and I slammed the book shut. I didn't want anyone to see what I'd written, and I wasn't going to tell anyone.

Inside my mind was just chitter-chatter: "Who do you think you are? You're just a lawyer. Bob Proctor doesn't even know you. What about your 401(k) and your equity partnership?" All this chatter was telling me why I shouldn't want what I really wanted.

I went ahead and I made a decision: I loved this idea so much that I was going to carry it out. I talked to the seminar room before I left after the weekend was over and said, "I don't know how, but I'm going to do this, because this is what I really want to do for my life." Today, I'm 50 percent owner in the Proctor Gallagher Institute. Bob and I had a fantastic partnership—the best business partnership that I could imagine—with a fantastic team doing work that we love and helping people around the world.

Anything is possible if you really dive into this program in detail. Some of it might not be all fun and excitement. You just put your thinking cap on and really think about the concepts and steps we're talking about and how you can apply them in your life. Then anything is possible for you. In fact, you can create your own economy. Think about that. You can create your own economy with the Science of Getting Rich.

There could be a couple, both in the same house. One of them is living in the Great Depression, and the other is having the best economy of their life. How can that be? One is operating in harmony with the law: they have a beautiful image of what they want. They are emotionally involved with that idea, which changes the vibration they're in; it attracts to them all they need for that picture to be fulfilled in their life. They've created their own economy. The other person is thinking about everything on the negative side—why they can't do something?—and all the bad news that's out there.

Both of these people are right. Remember, everything is both good and bad, so you're right whichever perspective you take, but which side do you want to be on? Of course you want to be on the side that's going to get you the results you want.

If you follow this program and if you do the exercises and think about these ideas, your future is going to be absolutely beautiful.

Everyone wants freedom. Why do we want it so badly? Because we're spiritual beings. Spirit is for expansion, freedom, fuller expression. We want to express our heart's desire; we want to express a greater part of ourselves. That is what we crave.

We crave time and money freedom. As I think back to my early lawyer days, when I was working on Wall Street, I see we had no time or money freedom. We were making good money, but it was just a grind. My colleagues and I didn't know a different way.

"Remember, everything is both good and bad, so you're right whichever perspective you take, but which side do you want to be on?"

That's why we need to have awareness. You'll be amazed at how much free time you have when you never have to think about money (which most people are continually doing). Even when I was making a high six-figure income, I was thinking about how I could make more. How could I provide more service? How could I help more people? I kept hitting a wall. I kept thinking, "I've got to put in more hours," because lawyers bill by the hour, and there are only so many hours in the day. My awareness wasn't at the point where I could see a different way.

Your level of awareness is everything. Your ability to get rich depends on it. If you don't change it, you will not change the results in your life. Awareness and consciousness are absolutely everything.

Think of consciousness as a dot. If we expand our awareness just a little, we can see how it turns into an expanding circle. That's your world expanding. Look how much bigger your world becomes. Just a little change, and your world expands dramatically.

We gain awareness through experiences. Everything we see, smell, taste, touch, and hear, expands our awareness. The experience you'll have with this book

---

"You expand your level of awareness
through effective education, combined
with top-notch professional coaching,
over a reasonable period of time."

---

will expand your awareness with a new way of thinking. When you get into this material, which presents deep wisdom methodically and scientifically, you'll have huge growth in your life.

Our objective is to constantly expand our awareness. Think of it this way: If a person is earning $100,000 a year, and they want to earn $100,000 a month, how do they do it? They have to gain awareness. They don't earn $100,000 a year because they want to; they earn $100,000 a year because they're not aware of how to earn $100,000 a month. Do you think if they became aware of how to earn $100,000 a month, they'd say, "I think I'll stick to $100,000 a year"? No way. Why not? Because we're spiritual beings, and spirit is for expansion and fuller expression.

We want to be of more service. We want to do more good. If we turn our annual income of $100,000 a year into $100,000 a month, that gives us another million plus to do more good. You can do a lot of good with a million dollars.

How do you expand your level of awareness? Through effective education, combined with top-notch professional coaching, over a reasonable period of time. You want to keep studying every single day. Let your awareness build and build: it's going to increase your knowledge of how to earn money as well.

I had a good education. I learned a lot. After I graduated from law school, I put in twenty-two years as a lawyer. I got the American Jurisprudence Award as the number one banking law student in the country. I worked for the top firms on Wall Street. I had a great, successful practice.

Did I have success? Sure. But if I look at those twenty-two years and compare them to the fifteen years of studying this material in partnership with Bob Proctor, my lawyer years pale in comparison. Since then, my income has multiplied incredibly. My lifestyle is far bigger and more beautiful than it was—deep friendships all over the world, working with a wonderful team every day. I love it. It all has come through discipline, study, and raising awareness. If you really get into this program, you'll see some beautiful results in your life.

It's a sad thing when a child is afraid of the dark. You know what? A lot of adults are afraid of the light, and that's even sadder. They don't even know what they're afraid of.

We don't want to be afraid of light. We want to keep bringing more light, eliminating the darkness, and expanding our awareness.

Here's a great truth: *everything that you are seeking is seeking you.* When Bob first said that, I thought, "What is he talking about?" Think about it this way: if you get emotionally involved with an idea, you impress it as a big, beautiful image of what you want on your subconscious mind. You thereby change your vibration and attract to you what you need. You are seeking a great goal, and it's attracting back to you what you need, so everything you're seeking is seeking you. It's all about induction and resonance.

Again, the trick to leading the life you want is awareness, and we want to work to expand it. The truth is that most people won't do the work. But if you do, if you commit time each day to expanding your awareness and to studying material that gives you good ideas that you can work with in your life, you can never lose. In fact, you'll be greatly rewarded.

It all starts with decisions. Throughout this entire book, you'll be called on to make decisions. You're going to ask yourself, "Do I want to do this? Do I want to invest in that? Do I want to pursue that goal?" Incredible awareness-raising information is going to fly into your mind, and the ideas are going to be flying like crazy. When I was in that first seminar, I felt overwhelmed: it

> Some tips to get the most from this book:
> - Commit time each day to expanding your awareness and studying the content.
> - Make decisions on the ideas quickly and change them very infrequently (if at all).
> - Open your mind and let the ideas go in deep.
> - Ask yourself: What do you want? What do you really want?

was as if I was vibrating at a completely different level. Even as I was sitting in the seminar room, my mind would float through boardrooms and executive offices, exploring how I would create a program.

This is going to happen to you. You're going to ask yourself to make decisions. Make them quickly, and don't go back and change your mind. You want to make decisions quickly and change them very infrequently, if at all. That's one of the great keys to success.

I made that decision in that seminar in Vancouver, Washington, on August 18, 2006. I am so grateful I did, and I've never gone back. There's huge power in that.

You want to make decisions, make them quickly, and set out to live the life that you truly want to live. I am so grateful that in 2006, I got to meet Bob Proctor and ultimately go into business partnership with him. He was an incredible human being.

Open your mind and let these ideas go in deep. When I opened my mind and I listened to Bob say, "What do you want? What do you really want?" I let my imagination fly, made decisions, and did tough things. The payoff was huge, and I want the same thing for you.

Chapter One

Getting Rich Is Your Right— and Your Duty

When Lloyd Conant gave me that first copy of *The Science of Getting Rich*, my world changed entirely. I started to study and understand something that most people never understand; it remains a puzzle through their entire life.

As you go through this book, you're going to hit on some ideas, and you're going to think your way out of the box. You may find yourself asking, "This is nuts. Does he really believe this?"

We not only believe it, we *are* it. We live these ideas all the time. I get up very early in the morning, at 5:00 or 5:30. I start my study period, and I don't stop, because I know that we're dealing with an infinite source of supply.

As it says in the Bible, "With all thy getting get understanding" (Proverbs 4:7). I don't care how great your understanding is; it can get better.

Understanding is the polar opposite of doubt and worry. If you're worrying and you have doubts about yourself, get understanding: that's where it's at. In all your getting, get understanding. You will attract it as you saturate your mind with this material; you move into that vibration.

Attraction is a secondary law. It's not a primary law. One primary law is the law of vibration, which decrees, "Everything moves; nothing rests." All the objects in the room you're in appear to be still, but they're moving; in fact, they're moving so fast, they appear to be still. Your entire body is moving at such a rapid clip—at the rate of 40 million cells per second—that it too appears to be still. (You can actually photograph the energy leaving the body. Way back in 1934, in Russia, Semyon Kirlian perfected a form of photography that could do that.) We have to understand that this whole universe is operating by law, not by accident.

When I started to study this information back in 1961, I was unhappy, I was sick, I was broke. I had two months of high school, I had a bad work record, and I had a bad attitude. Yet I had the audacity to say that the authors of these books were crazy.

We tend to criticize or ridicule anything we don't understand. Back in the early days, I couldn't explain anything that these people were saying, so I would say it's crazy, and I would throw it away.

At this point, I recommend that you get a pad and pen and write this down: *Don't reject anything.*

Now write underneath: *Don't accept anything.* You don't have to reject something; nor do you have to accept it. The beautiful truth is, you and I have the ability to choose. You may not want to accept an idea, but don't reject it. Consider it. Think about it. Thinking is the highest function that we're capable of, but unfortunately we don't do enough of it.

Reject nothing. Listen to everything. That doesn't mean you have to accept it. Think about it, consider it.

Authors Stewart Edward White and Harwood White have observed that it's curious how we acquire wisdom. Over and over again, the same truth is thrust under our very nose. We read it in the written word. We suffer the experiences they describe. We gradually assent to the advice, we approve intellectually, but nothing happens inside of us. Then one day, some trivial experience or word or encounter stops us short. A gleam of illumination penetrates the depths of our consciousness. A brilliant flash reveals truth fully formed, and we marvel that the understanding has escaped us for so long.

If nothing happens inside, nothing's going to happen outside. If you want your bank account to grow, you've got to change inside. If you want to have a more lov-

Bob Proctor's Rules for Studying This Book:
1. Don't reject anything
2. Don't accept anything
3. Listen to everything
4. Think about and consider everything
5. Apply the ideas that make sense to you.

ing relationship, you've got to change inside. If you want your business to grow, you've got to change inside.

Napoleon Hill spent his whole life studying 500 of the world's most accomplished individuals. He took what he learned and he wrote the laws of achievement. From these laws, he created the book *Think and Grow Rich*. He presented the essence of the best thinking of 500 of the world's most accomplished individuals from 1908 to 1937—people like Henry Ford, King Gillette, and Thomas Edison. Even so, no amount of reading or memorizing is going to make you successful; it's the understanding and application of wise thoughts.

Lloyd C. Douglas wrote a book called *The Magnificent Obsession*. I thought, how could an obsession be magnificent? I thought it was a negative thing. That caused me to go and look up the word. Here's the definition of obsession: "a persistent, disturbing preoccupation with an often unreasonable idea."

"Obsession: A persistent, disturbing preoccupation with an often unreasonable idea."
—Lloyd C. Douglas

That can be very positive.

There's no end to what you're capable of doing—absolutely none. Your spiritual DNA is perfect. What do I mean by that? You're God's highest form of creation. There is nothing on the planet that will even come close to you.

All the other creatures on the planet are completely at home in their environment, but we're totally disoriented. We don't blend in because we have been given the god-like ability to create our own environment. We've been given higher faculties. We have mental faculties that, so far as we know, no other form of life has.

We were created in God's image. There's perfection in us. It's the core of your being and consciousness, and that perfection is forever seeking expression within and through you. It wants to express itself in a greater way. That's why you always want more. It's not that you're greedy. It's not that you don't have enough. You want more because the essence of who you are wants to express itself in a greater way. If you run, you want to run faster; if you jump, you want to jump higher; if you're selling, you want to sell more.

You often hear people say that they're spiritual beings having a physical experience. That's what you're having in this lifetime.

Here's what separates us from all the rest of the animal kingdom: we have an intellect. Through the proper use of the intellect, we can control and change our emotions. The intellect activates the emotions.

Now look at spirit. Where is it? Go to any of the great spiritual classics—the Bhagavad Gita, the Koran, the Torah, the Bible, the Book of Mormon. They'll all tell you spirit is everywhere. Spirit is evenly present in all places at all times. Where's God? God is everywhere.

Wernher von Braun, the father of the US space program, was probably one of the greatest scientists that ever lived. He said that years of studying the spectacular mysteries of the cosmos led him to a firm belief in the existence of God. He said the natural laws of this universe are so precise that we don't have any difficulty building spaceships, sending people to the moon, and timing the landing within a fraction of a second. He said these laws must have been set by somebody.

The highest side of your personality is the spiritual side. The lowest side is the physical side. Here's what we want to try and understand. You have been gifted with an intellect, which enables you to change the world. Every vibratory frequency is hooked up to the one above and

> **The highest side of your personality
> is the spiritual side. The lowest side
> is the physical side.**

the one below. We can tap into a higher level to change a lower level. No other form of life can do that.

Here is another concept. If I take some water and heat it, what's going to happen? The water is going to stop being water, and it's going to start being steam. You don't even call it water anymore. If we continue to add heat, the steam turns into air, or gas. Just as steam is on a higher level than water, air is on a higher level than steam. They're all connected.

That's one of the first laws of the universe: the perpetual transmutation of energy. Energy is forever moving into form, through form, and out of form. You can do it yourself. Here you are, a spiritual being, you have an intellect, and you live in a physical body. What is the highest function that we're capable of? Thinking. Like spirit, thoughts are omnipresent. You can think underwater, in the air, or walking down the street. As you think, you pull thoughts together to build ideas.

If you look at any object, you can see that at one time, it was nothing but an idea. A goal is also an idea. If I hold that idea long enough, it must move into form. That is an absolute law of being. It's a beautiful concept, yet most people miss it.

You've got to change your mind if you want to change your results. You've got to change your mind if you want to change your bank account. Mind is in every molecule of your being. It's as much in your fingernail as it is in your brain. Mind is movement. The body is a manifestation of that movement: the body is the instrument of the mind.

We can say that the mind is divided into two parts: the conscious and the subconscious. The conscious mind is the part of you that thinks. That's also where your intellect resides.

With your conscious mind, you have the ability to think whatever you choose. Viktor Frankl, a Jewish psychiatrist, spent the years of World War II in a Nazi concentration camp. He wrote a famous book about his experiences entitled *Man's Search for Meaning*. He said that regardless of the abuse he was subjected to, no one could cause him to think something he didn't want to think.

That's true for you too. No one can cause you to think something you don't want to think. You have the ability to choose. The subconscious is the emotional mind. It's quite different from the conscious mind. Unlike the latter, it cannot reject: it must accept the thoughts that are presented to it. It's like the earth, which will grow what you plant regardless of what it is. In his famous recording

"The Strangest Secret," inspirational speaker Earl Nightingale said that you can plant corn, a sweet food, or you can plant nightshade, a deadly poison. One will grow in just as great abundance as the other. Your subconscious mind cannot differentiate between what's real and what's imagined.

Since, with our conscious mind, we have the ability to think what we choose, let's say you want to change your life. What do you do? You think of exactly how you want to live.

Write out exactly how you want to live in all areas of your life. Make a written description of it in the present tense. When you pass that idea to the subconscious mind, it doesn't know that this is just an image. It accepts it as real. You've got this beautiful image written in the present tense. When you impress it upon your subconscious mind, you move into a vibration whereby you'll attract everything that is in harmony with that image.

Today you've got lots of information flying into your conscious mind from the social media, from other peo-

Write out exactly how you want
to live in all areas of your life. Make
a written description in the present tense
and focus on it. Then the subconscious
mind will act on the image as real.

ple, from TV, from newspapers. But you still have the power to think: you can say, "I don't want any of that information. I don't want any of that stuff."

The problem is, we don't do that. Why? Because we don't think; we leave our mind wide open. All this negativity is going right into our subconscious mind, which does not have the ability to reject it, so that's the vibration we're in.

Now why do we do that? We're programmed to live this way. We do so because of a paradigm, which is a multitude of habits that are fixed in our subconscious mind.

We did not build this paradigm ourselves. It was built into us when we were little. When we're infants, what's going on around us goes right into our subconscious mind, because it's wide open. That's why we learn the language of the people we're surrounded by as infants. If you were born into an English-speaking family, and you were taken out of that home as an infant and moved into a suburb of Beijing, you would grow up fluent in Chinese, with no knowledge of English. Why? Because you'd be surrounded by people that only speak Chinese.

Whatever you're surrounded by goes into your subconscious mind. I was born in 1934, during the Great Depression, when there was nothing but lack and limitation. Then, when I was just a little kid in school, the Second World War came along, and everything was rationed. All this lack and limitation were being programmed into my subconscious mind.

Do you know that you have an image of yourself that was built way back, when you were an infant? You didn't choose that image; somebody else built it for you. You may not have built it, you may not be responsible for it, but you *are* responsible for changing it. If you've got limitations in there, you didn't build them yourself, but you've got to change them. And we're quite capable of changing.

A paradigm is a mental program that has almost exclusive control over our habitual behavior. Almost all of our behavior is habitual. We're programmed in our subconscious mind to think and live the way we do.

A paradigm is a mental program that has almost exclusive control over our habitual behavior.

Now here's what I want to ask you: look at your results. If your results aren't that good, let's make up our minds to change them.

At a very early age, we go to school. School gives us very valuable knowledge, but it teaches us virtually nothing about paradigms; therefore we do not do what we already know how to do. Although we've got the knowledge in our conscious mind, the paradigms are controlling our behavior. We have superior knowledge, but inferior results, and that causes confusion and frustration.

Some people are absolutely brilliant, but their results are terrible. They're really bright, but they're broke. They're very smart, but they don't know how to build relationships with other people. Their knowledge isn't controlling their lives; their paradigms are. If they want to change their results, they've got to change their paradigms.

Your conscious mind, your intellectual mind, will determine whether you change your paradigm or not. The intellectual mind controls the emotional mind. The emotional mind in turn dictates the vibration you're in, and that controls what you attract to you.

Our intellectual factors include perception, will, imagination, memory, intuition, and reason. Here's the problem: we were taught nothing about them in school. You have all these magnificent faculties in your conscious mind, you can call on them and use them to change your vibration, but we don't even know they're there.

Whatever may be said in praise of poverty, the fact remains that it is not possible to live a really complete or successful life unless one is rich. People may disagree, saying you don't need money to be happy. But that's not what I'm saying here. I said that it's not possible to live a really complete or successful life unless one is rich. We cannot rise to our greatest possible height or talent in soul development unless we have plenty of money. In order to unfold the soul and develop talent, we must have many things to use. We cannot have these things unless we have the money to buy them with.

The essence of you is spirit. Spirit is perfect, and spirit is always for expansion and fuller expression. We cannot rise to our greatest possible height unless we have plenty of money. People develop in mind, soul, and body by making use of things, and society is so organized that people must have money in order to possess things. That's what commerce is all about. Money is a medium, and we exchange it for other people's products or services.

Each of us has the right to life. This means the right to have the free and unrestricted use of all the things that may be necessary for our fullest mental, spiritual, and physical unfolding—in other words, the right to be rich. We've got a right to be rich.

To be really rich does not mean to be satisfied or contented with a little. You may say, "I don't need all this to get by." No, you don't. Squirrels come up to our door in the morning for almonds that we throw to them. I don't want to live like squirrels. I don't want to wait for somebody to throw something out to me. I want to live a dignified life, and I want to live an abundant life, and I want to be philanthropic in all my thoughts and everything I do. I want to help everybody. If you have the ability, why not?

To be really rich does not mean to be satisfied or contented with a little when you're capable of using and enjoying more. The purpose of nature is the advancement or development of life. I believe we're here to do God's work. God's work is greater goodness. God's purpose is expansion, expression, and greater good. If you're here to do God's work, you're here to do greater good.

Are you doing greater good? Are you satisfied with not doing the greater good that you could do because you're short of money? Earn more. Everybody can earn more money. There's no end. All the money in the world is available to you; all you have to do is earn it. The purpose of nature is advancement and development of life. Every individual should have all they can use to contribute to the power, elegance, beauty, and richness of life. When you own all you want for the living all the life that you are capable of living, you are rich.

You cannot have all you want without plenty of money. Life has advanced so far and become so complex that even the most ordinary man or woman requires a great amount of wealth in order to live in a manner that even approaches completeness. You naturally want to become all that you're capable of becoming.

This desire to realize any and all possibilities is inherent in human nature. There's something in you that wants you to grow. People who are not doing all they're capable of doing are very frustrated. You've got to find an expression for your talent. You've got to find an expression for what you're capable of doing.

I believe that every one of us is hardwired to do something very well. I believe you are talented. You've got a talent within you, and if you're not utilizing it, you're not enjoying your life.

There are three motives for which we live. We live for the body, the mind, and the soul. No one of these is better than the other. Each is desirable, and neither body, mind, nor soul can live fully if one of the others is cut short of life or expression. It is not right or noble to live only for the soul and deny the mind or body. Vows of poverty don't make any sense to me. Similarly, it's wrong to live for the intellect and deny the body or the soul. We have to live for all areas. In chapter 1 of *The Science of Getting Rich*, Wallace Wattles writes:

> It is perfectly right that you should desire to be rich; if you are a normal man or woman you cannot help doing so. It is perfectly right that you should give your best attention to the Science of Getting Rich, for it is the noblest and most necessary of all studies. If you neglect this study, you are derelict in your duty to yourself, to God, and to humanity; for you can render God and humanity no greater service than to make the most of yourself.

Do you want to do something for the world? Bring the best out of yourself. Be the very best that you can be at what you do.

Application exercises for the three motives for which we live:

1. *The body*—Write out a description of your ideal body, from both a health and physical standpoint.

2. *The mind*—How is your memory? How creative are you? Write out three ideas for how you could improve your mental abilities.

3. *The soul*—Write out a clear description of the types of activities which give your soul a deep sense of satisfaction, and make you feel alive.

Chapter Two

Working with the Laws

There is a Science of getting rich, and it is an exact science, like algebra or arithmetic. There are certain laws which govern the process of acquiring riches; once these laws are learned and obeyed by any man, he will get rich with mathematical certainty.
—The Science of Getting Rich

The law of attraction was made famous by Rhonda Byrne's film *The Secret* in 2006. As soon as it came out, people starting writing books on the law of attraction, although they didn't really understand it; very few people really do in depth.

Actually, attraction is a secondary law. There's one great law. According to theology, that one great law is—

God IS. God is neither created or destroyed, is the cause and effect of itself, is 100% evenly present in all places at the same time. According to science, the same law is stated as Energy Is.

All physical and mental science is based on this one great law and its seven subsidiary laws, which operate in coordination with each other.

The Seven Primary Laws of the Universe
• Vibration
• Perpetual transmutation
• Relativity
• Polarity
• Rhythm
• Cause and Effect
• Gender

Vibration is one of these primary laws. Everything moves; nothing rests. Do you know that a body in a coffin is moving? You'll say, "Come on. It's dead." Nothing is dead. Nothing is created or destroyed. Everything is in a constant evolution of change.

Think. If the body in the coffin weren't moving, how would it ever change to dust? Vibration is constant. The walls in the room you're in are moving. They appear to be still, but nothing is still. Everything is moving. We live in an ocean of motion.

For this reason, the thoughts that I think, particularly those that I'm emotionally involved with, will dictate the vibration I'm in. I can only attract to me that which vibrates in harmony with me. If I'm in a negative vibration, I'm going to attract bad things. If I'm in a good vibration, I'm going to attract good things.

At one point, President John Kennedy asked Werner von Braun, "What would it take to build a rocket that will carry a person to the moon and bring him back safely to earth?" Von Braun replied, "The will to do it."

> A fateful conversation with President Kennedy:
>
> President John Kennedy: "What would it take to build a rocket that will carry a person to the moon and bring him back safely to earth?"
>
> Wernher Von Braun: "The *will* to do it."

The will is the mental faculty that enables you to hold one idea on the screen of your mind to the exclusion of all outside distractions. Most people can't hold one idea on the screen of their mind for more than a second or two, but it's a skill you can acquire.

Here's one technique. Put a little dot on the wall opposite your favorite chair. (Don't tell anybody you've done it. If somebody sees it, they'll just take it for a fly on the wall.) When you're sitting in that chair, concentrate on that dot. You focus on the dot. Don't let your mind leave the dot. By doing that, you develop your will.

Next is the law of **perpetual transmutation**. Energy is always moving, and it's always moving into form, through form, and back out of form. With our bodies, we moved into form, and we're going to move through form.

Then comes **relativity**. Everything's relative. Nothing's big, nothing's small. Train yourself to think this way: if you think earning $1 million is a lot of money, sit down, take your pen, and figure out how to earn $2 million. Then $1 million is going to look small. It looks big because you're relating it to, say, $50,000, $150,000. You've got to make it look small.

One day I was talking to personal development expert Peggy McColl. She said that she and her husband were out looking at houses. She saw one that she really liked, but it was $1 million more than they wanted to pay. I said, "Make the million look small." Within a couple of days, I had a book cover in my email from Peggy. The book was called *Make a Million Look Small*.

Then we have the law of **polarity**. It decrees that everything has an opposite. There would be no inside to your house if there weren't an outside.

I have a desk in my studio. It's about three feet, six inches high. It's only a short way up onto that desk, so it's only a short way down. It couldn't be a short way up and a long way down. Equal and opposite—the law of polarity.

There is the law of **rhythm**. There are highs and lows, and the pendulum swings back and forth between them. The tide goes out, the tide comes in. The night follows the day. Biorhythm affects you on all levels, intellectually, emotionally, and physically.

Some days you're at a peak intellectually. On other days, you're on a low: you can't remember anything or figure anything out. Some days you may be adding up a column of figures. You do it five times and get a different answer every time. Other times, you get the answer right away, on the button.

When you're on a high emotionally, you want to skip down the street, help an old lady across the road, and pat a little kid on the head. On other days—"What is that old lady doing out there? Get that kid out of here!" Physically, there are times when your body feels as if it's dragging; other times, you're as sharp as a tack.

Then there's the law of **cause and effect**. Every cause has an effect, and every effect becomes a cause that has an effect in turn. We call this a train of causation. Moreover, whatever you put out comes back. If you're providing a lot of service, you're going to get a lot of reward.

Then you have the law of **gender**. The law of gender decrees that all seeds have a gestation period. When you plant a seed, a period of time must elapse for that seed to manifest and form. The gestation period for babies is about 280 days.

These are basic laws. All the other laws are offshoots of it: they are secondary laws. If you study these laws and live in harmony with them to the best of your ability, you're going to win.

The best definition of *natural law* seems to be that it is the uniform and orderly method of the omnipotent God. In other words, it's God's modus operandi. Unlike the other forms of life that have been created, we were given the power of choice or free will. Along with this power came certain responsibility.

Put a big circle around this paragraph, because it's very important. *The capacity to choose does not involve freedom from that choice.* In other words, if you make a mistake, you're going to pay. You can say, "But I didn't know." Tough. It's the law. If you do something wrong, you're going to get it back. The laws are always working, and they have a beautiful way of evening things out.

We are subject to the law. If we don't understand the law, we're going to be screwing up right and left. Don't look at the law as bad. Look at it as necessary to help us get to where we're going.

"The capacity to choose does not involve
freedom from the consequences of that choice."
—Bob Proctor

The capacity to choose does not involve freedom from the consequences of our choice. The laws that govern every individual are as exact as those that govern the material universe. You can act in accordance with these laws or you can disregard them, but you cannot in any way alter them. You will never change the laws. I don't care how much power you're given, what your position is, or how much money you have. You cannot change the law. You are subject to the law. If you live in harmony with it, good for you; you're going to win.

The law forever operates and holds you to strict accountability, and there is not the slightest allowance for ignorance. The law of attraction will deliver to you what you do *not* want as quickly and as certainly as it will deliver what you do want. If you're spending time thinking about what you don't want, you're going to get it, as surely as it's going to get dark tonight.

Wattles' comments:

The ownership of money and property comes as a result of doing things in a certain way; those who do things in this Certain Way, whether on purpose or accidentally, get rich; while those who do not do things in this Certain Way, no matter how hard they work or how able they are, remain poor.

It is a natural law that like causes always produce like effects; and, therefore, any man or woman who learns to do things in this Certain Way will infallibly get rich. . . .

Getting rich is not a matter of environment, for, if it were, all the people in certain neighborhoods would become wealthy; the people of one city would all be rich, while those of other towns would all be poor; or the inhabitants of one state would roll in wealth, while those of an adjoining state would be in poverty.

But everywhere we see rich and poor living side by side, in the same environment, and often engaged in the same vocations. When two men are in the same locality, and in the same business, and one gets rich while the other remains poor, it shows that getting rich is not, primarily, a matter of environment. Some environments may be more favorable than others, but when two men in the same business are in the same neighborhood, and one gets rich while the other fails, it indicates that getting rich is the result of doing things in a Certain Way.

If you're living in a welfare area, you're probably not going to be exposed to a lot of high-powered creative thinking. But if you're living in the richest part of town, you could still be involved in some terrible thinking, and in that case, you're going to lose.

Some people who are doing very well have no understanding of these concepts at all, but still they act in such a way that they become rich. They're called *unconscious competents*. They don't understand what they're doing, but their paradigm is programmed to live in harmony with these laws. Their subconscious mind is helping them make it, but they're not quite sure what's going on. Many people have come to my seminars and said, "I've been doing that for a long time." They just weren't aware that they were acting in harmony with the laws.

As we really get into this material, we're going to find that it works like unadulterated magic. The paradigm is the demon. That's what's holding us back. It's a mental program that has almost exclusive control over our habitual behavior, and almost all of our behavior is habitual.

Your paradigm affects many areas in your life. It affects your perception. You're going to find that your perception is a very big tool. If you change your perception, everything changes. My late friend Wayne Dyer put it very well: "When you change the way you look at something, what you look at changes," and he's so right.

Your paradigm controls how you use your time, and it controls your creativity. Everybody's creative; no one is more creative than anyone else. Some merely express their creativity to a greater degree than others.

Your paradigm also controls your effectiveness. As I keep improving my paradigm, I become more effective. The more effective you are, the more productive you're going to be. We should always be raising the bar.

Then there's the role of logic in your paradigm. We're programmed to let logic stop us. It's almost as if we have a wall built around us. Every time we go to change something, the wall stops us. But when we decide to change the paradigm, the wall comes down.

If you start consciously and deliberately working in harmony with law, the change is not only going to be huge, it will be permanent, and it will keep getting better. If you change your perception and bring it into harmony with the law, your income will skyrocket. That's just the way it works.

The Danish philosopher Søren Kierkegaard said, "We can only get in touch with our own source of intuition and wisdom when we no longer depend upon others' opinions for our sense of identity or worth. We all tend to worship something. The question is, will we worship the God of opinion or the God of our heart? I found I had less and less to say, until finally, I became silent and began to listen. I discovered in the silence the voice of God."

"The question is, will we worship the God
of opinion or the God of our heart?"
—Soren Kierkegaard

Spirit talks to you through your intuitive factor. If you want to solve a problem, ask the universe, ask spirit for the answer. The answer's going to come, but you've got to be receptive to it. Your intuitive factor gives you the answer. It's a feeling that "I just got it." That's what Kierkegaard is talking about here.

Let's look at the laws in more detail. The law of perpetual transmutation—what do we mean by that? We mean that law is forever moving into form. You have the spiritual world, the intellectual world, and the physical world. You go from the higher to the lower.

What's the highest form in our mind? The highest form is thoughts. Thoughts turn into an idea on the intellectual level, and if we hold that idea long enough, it will ultimately move into form. That's the perpetual transmutation of energy. The idea moves into form, and it moves from a higher to a lower state. When you're working with energy, you're always working from a higher to a lower state.

You know what we do? We work from the lower to the higher. We look at the outside; we let results control our thinking. Go to thought, and let it control your results. That's the perpetual transmutation of energy.

As we get our thoughts to move into form, we have the law of relativity. Say you have three barrels: A, B, and C. Now is B big or small? It's neither. B just is. B is only big if you compare it to A. It's only small if you relate it to C. Whenever you're dealing with something you think is too big, come up with something bigger and relate it to that: make it small. Reduce it to the ridiculous, and you'll know you can step out and make it happen.

Three Barrels—Big or Small?

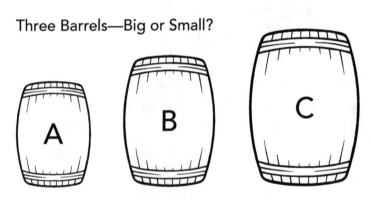

The law of vibration decrees that everything's moving. With our marvelous mind, we can pick up that vibration. Everything we attract, we attract through the law of vibration. Our vibration will dictate what we attract.

The Science of Getting Rich has to do with energy. Energy functions on frequencies. A frequency is a level of vibration. There's an infinite number of frequencies. We can only attract according to the frequency we're on.

If I dial your number on the phone, how do I get you on the other end? Because we're both on the same frequency. Match the frequency of the reality you want, and you cannot help but create that reality. It can be no other way. This is not philosophy. It's physics.

Because everything's energy, the money you want is energy. The building you want, the business you want—they're all energy. If you think you're going to have trouble and you let something outside dictate where you're going to go, you're going to have trouble, and the outside is indeed going to dictate where you'll go. But if you know that you build the image in your mind, you put yourself on the right frequency, and you act like what you want to become, then you get it. That's just the way it works.

Here's a good way of looking at the law of polarity. This is an effective step for staying in control of your life regardless of what happens. If we're looking at a situation in life, and it's only a little bad, when we work our way around to the other side, it's only going to be a little good. It's just a little problem, so there's only a little win in it. Any sharp consultant who goes into a company is looking for a big problem, because when we find a big problem, there is a big solution, and it brings about a big win.

Here is a great three-step process to follow in order to use the law of polarity. It's from minister and spiritual director Michael Beckwith.

1. Whatever it is, accept it. It's either going to control you, or you're going to control it.

2. Harvest the good. The more good you look for, the more you're going to find. There's good in everything. God is good all the time.

3. Forgive all the rest. Just forgive it. Let it go, completely let go.

This is a great way of utilizing the law of polarity.

Now let's look at the law of rhythm. There are times in your life when you feel you're living on a roller coaster. This is the way the law of rhythm works. There are highs, and there are lows.

Now here's what we want to understand: everybody's subject to this law. No one gets special dispensation. No one's exempt—not the wisest or the wealthiest. You don't get out of it.

Understand that when you're on a low swing, there's something good coming. It'll be better tomorrow. Start to expect the best, because that's the way it works. Highs always follows lows. Summer always follows winter. Winter never follows winter.

Now let's look at the law of gender, which states that everything has its masculine and its feminine principles. All creation has both male and female energy. Regardless of sexual preference, men have a feminine side, women

> "All things have both the yin, feminine,
> and the yang, masculine, energy.
> Yin is the passive, receptive energy,
> while yang is the active energy."

have a masculine side, and everyone would benefit from learning more about this other side of the self.

Because we are all made of energy, the law of gender relates to energy dynamics. This concept of male and female energy is very similar to the Chinese concept of the yin and yang. All things have both the yin, feminine, and the yang, masculine, energy. Yin is the passive, receptive energy, while yang is the active energy. Like the law of gender, the teaching of yin-yang explains that opposites are complementary. The Chinese use this system for everything, and it is interesting to explore how yin and yang energies interact to balance each other. For example, when ingested, a more yin vegetable can balance a more yang person.

The law of cause and effect is one that everyone should learn. Everything you do is a cause. Know that when you're doing something that it's a cause, so make damn sure it's for good.

Forget about getting even. One time I was talking to a guy who had been involved in the mob. He said, "You know, Bob, in our business, when you have a partner, you stick up for your partner. You let no one say anything bad about your partner. But if your partner double-crosses you, you kill him."

I got to thinking about it afterwards and decided that that's not a bad idea. I don't mean take a gun and shoot someone. But if people double-cross you, kill them mentally. Have nothing more to do with them. That's how I live. Certain people have not treated me right in the past. It's all over. I'm not interested in getting even, but I'm not going to let them make another run at the same thing.

There's a cause-and-effect relationship in every-thing in life. Make certain that you put the best out in every situation. Do the best you know how to do under every circumstance. There we have the apothecary's scale: service and reward. The law of cause and effect operates in everything. It's important to understand it and follow it.

The law of compensation is based on the law of cause and effect. The law of compensation is very clear. If you want to earn more money, you'd better understand this law. If you don't, you're going to lose. It states that the amount of money you earn will always be in exact ratio to the need for what you do, your ability to do it, and the difficulty of replacing you. If you get very good at something, if you master what you're doing, you're going to be very difficult to replace. When you become difficult to replace, your stock goes up, and you automatically start doing better financially. It's all based on the law of cause and effect.

Study and learn to live in harmony with all of these laws. Dig into them.

The Seven Primary Laws of the Universe:
- Vibration
- Perpetual transmutation
- Relativity
- Polarity
- Rhythm
- Cause and Effect
- Gender

Chapter Three

The First Principle

Much of the material in this book is, as I've said, based on Wallace D. Wattles' classic *The Science of Getting Rich*. One of the most important parts is chapter 4: "The First Principle in the Science of Getting Rich."

The chapter begins, "Thought is the only power which can produce tangible riches from the Formless Substance. The stuff from which all things are made is a substance which thinks, and a thought of form in this substance produces the form."

To the average person's way of thinking, that's so far out of the box that it seems ridiculous. But as you start to work with this principle, it starts to make a great deal of sense.

Take two people: A and B. (You could say that these are my lives prior to age twenty-six and after). They both have infinite potential, and they both have the ability to choose. B wanders around back and forth and nowhere.

The results are mediocre. Nothing's happening. On the other side, with A, it's prosperity, satisfaction, happiness, continuous growth. Both started out evenly with the same talents and abilities.

The difference? One is being controlled by a paradigm, the other is controlling the paradigm. Up until now, you may have been controlled by your paradigm. If you don't like the results you've been getting and you've been going along for a long time, you've probably been controlled by your paradigm. Make up your mind that you're going to change that.

To go a step further, A has a goal and believes that it will manifest. That's the difference right there. B has a paradigm problem.

Science fiction writer Robert A. Heinlein said, "In the absence of clearly defined goals, we become strangely loyal to performing daily trivia until ultimately we become enslaved by it." I work around sales organizations, and with some people I see no real change in results. They are much the same week after week, month after month. What's going on? These people are involved in daily trivia, to which they ultimately become enslaved. They're talking about things that make no difference and are not going to serve them, and they're not going in the direction they want to go in. Whereas others achieve prosperity, satisfaction, happiness, and continuous growth.

"In the absence of clearly defined goals, we become strangely loyal to performing daily trivia until ultimately we become enslaved by it."
—Robert A. Heinlein

Here's what I do. Every morning at five o'clock, I sit down and write out things I'm grateful for. At the bottom, I write: *I am so happy and grateful now that I realize my spiritual DNA is perfect and that perfection is within me. I begin each day looking for areas of my life where I want to see that perfection expressed habitually.* Although I'm right-handed, I write that statement out at the bottom with my left hand. Why? It's very awkward. It feels very uncomfortable, and it helps me understand that if I'm really comfortable doing everything I'm doing, I'm probably not growing much. Then I start my study program.

B wouldn't do that. B would say, "First, I don't get up at that time. What's that about? That doesn't make any sense at all." It won't make any sense if you don't understand about paradigms, discipline, the mind, the rules for winning, or the value of goals. If you're going to reach your goal, you're going to have to do things that are uncomfortable at times, because you're going into areas where you have never been before.

You've got to develop awareness, and you've got to work on your paradigms. That's absolutely essential. If you're going to do that, you've got to focus on new results. Remember what Wattles wrote: "Thought is the only power which can produce tangible riches from the Formless Substance. The stuff from which all things are made is a substance which thinks, and a thought of form in this substance produces the form."

"The stuff from which all things are made." What things? The clothes you've got on, your body, the world you see around you.

Everything is made from this formless substance. You could take everything you own, throw it onto a big pile, and set a match to it. It would all go back to where it came from. It all comes from formless substance. But thought is the only power. There's power in thought, and you can think. We're the only form of life, so far as we know, that can think. Wattles says:

Original Substance moves according to its thoughts; every form and process you see in nature is the visible expression of a thought in Original Substance. As the Formless Stuff thinks of a form, it takes that form; as it thinks of a motion, it makes that motion. That is the way all things were created. We live in a thought world, which is part of a thought universe.

> "Original Substance moves according
> to it thoughts; every form and process
> you see in nature is the visible expression
> of a thought in Original Substance."
> —Wallace Wattles

In truth, there's no such thing as creation. Nothing is created or destroyed. In that case, how do we get things? Creation, as we know it, occurs when we cause one form of energy to make another form of energy. It creates something different, which would have never been created had you not originated that first thought form of energy. We're manipulating energy with our mind all the time. Wattles continues:

The thought of a moving universe extended throughout Formless Substance, and the Thinking Stuff moving according to that thought, took the form of systems of planets, and maintains that form. Thinking Substance takes the form of its thought, and moves according to the thought. Holding the idea of a circling system of suns and worlds, it takes the form of these bodies, and moves them as it thinks. Thinking the form of a slow-growing oak tree, it moves accordingly, and produces the tree, though centuries may be required to do the work. In creating, the Formless seems to move according to the lines of motion it has established; the thought of an oak tree does not cause the instant formation of a full-grown tree, but it does start in motion the forces which will produce the tree, along established lines of growth.

Every thought of form, held in Thinking Substance, causes the creation of the form, but always, or at least generally, along lines of growth and action already established.

The thought of a house of a certain construction, if it were impressed upon Formless Substance, might not cause the instant formation of the house; but it would cause the turning of creative energies already working in trade and commerce into such channels as to result in the speedy building of the house. And if there were no existing channels through which the creative energy could work, then the house would be formed directly from primal substance, without waiting for the slow processes of the organic and inorganic world.

If you think of building a house, all kinds of things are set in motion. Telepathic communication starts to take place. You start to activate thoughts in other people's minds. Suggestions will come to you. People will come to you. Things will happen. There's no question about it.

"You've got to create the picture of
what you want in your mind, and you've
got to stop letting the outside world
dictate what you want."
—Bob Proctor

Wattles goes on to say, *"No thought of form can be impressed upon Original Substance without causing the creation of that form."** You've got to create the picture of what you want in your mind, and you've got to stop letting the outside world dictate what you want. Quit looking at your bank account, for God's sake. Imagine your bank account. See what you want. Visualize it.

"Man is a thinking center, and can originate thought," Wattles writes. Tell me something else outside of a human being that can originate thought. There is not a thing else. You're it. I don't know what you've been thinking in the past, I don't know what you're thinking of yourself, but I do know this: if you can think it, you can do it. If you can hold it in your head, you can hold it in your hand. I don't care what it is.

"All the forms that man fashions with his hands must first exist in his thought; he cannot shape a thing until he has thought that thing," Wattles writes. It's like Van

* All emphasis in quoted material is from the original.

Gogh. The great artist was asked how he did such beautiful work. He said, "I dream my painting, and then I paint my dream."

Wattles continues:

> So far man has confined his efforts wholly to the work of his hands; he has applied manual labor to the world of forms, seeking to change or modify those already existing. He has never thought of trying to cause the creation of new forms by impressing his thoughts upon Formless Substance.
>
> When man has a thought-form, he takes material from the forms of nature, and makes an image of the form which is in his mind. He has, so far, made little or no effort to co-operate with Formless Intelligence; to work "with the Father." He has not dreamed that he can "do what he seeth the Father doing."

There's a formless intelligence. We're dealing with an intelligent power. Everything the Father can do, you can do. We've been taught this many ways. Our problem is, we don't believe it. Belief is the key.

> Man reshapes and modifies existing forms by manual labor; he has given no attention to the question whether

he may not produce things from Formless Substance by communicating his thoughts to it. We propose to prove that he may do so; to prove that any man or woman may do so, and to show how. As our first step, we must lay down three fundamental propositions.

First, we assert that there is one original formless stuff, or substance, from which all things are made. All the seemingly many elements are but different presentations of one element; all the many forms found in organic and inorganic nature are but different shapes, made from the same stuff. And this stuff is thinking stuff; a thought held in it produces the form of the thought. Thought, in thinking substance, produces shapes. Man is a thinking center, capable of original thought; if man can communicate his thought to original thinking substance, he can cause the creation, or formation, of the thing he thinks about. To summarize this:

There is a thinking stuff from which all things are made, and which, in its original state, permeates, penetrates, and fills the interspaces of the universe.

A thought, in this substance, produces the thing that is imaged by the thought.

Man can form things in his thought, and, by impressing his thought upon formless substance, can cause the thing he thinks about to be created. . . .

Reasoning back from the phenomenon of form and thought, I come to one original thinking substance; and reasoning forward from this thinking substance, I came to the individual power to cause the formation of the thing one thinks about.

And by experiment, I find this reasoning to be true; and this is my strongest proof.

If one man who listens to this program gets rich by doing what I say to do, that is evidence to support my claim; but if every man who does what it tells him to do gets rich, that is positive proof until some one goes through the process and fails. The theory is true until the process fails; and this process will not fail, for every man who does exactly what this book tells him to do will get rich.

Can you do it? Anybody can do it, but you've got to work from the inside out. We're talking about results. We're talking about making it happen. Results always tell the truth. Looking at your results, do you subscribe to what Wattles is talking about?

How do results happen? Results are thoughts that move into form. Do they just happen? I don't think so.

Let's take a closer look at results and how they happen. I want you to look at your results. What role does awareness play in our results? It plays an enormous role. It's where it all happens.

At one point, I was in the fire department. The first call I went on was very early in the morning, around four or five. A police officer was going down the street, and he saw a fire coming out of the windows of the third story of a house. He put a call in, and we went out.

There was a woman sleeping on the third floor. She lived in two rooms on the third floor, and she had a little boy. The little boy was in bed with her sleeping. The little boy got up and went into the kitchen. He got into the cupboard, got a big box of matches, and started playing with it. He set the matches off and boom! The whole box went up in flames.

The boy got scared, dropped the matches, and got back into bed. Needless to say, the third floor of that place was burning up. We got the fire trucks there and put the fire out. That little boy could have easily died because he was not aware of the dangers of fire. That's where the lack of awareness comes in.

Awareness is not a high enough priority when we teach children. In fact, it's taken second place to the intellect. School is all about developing intellectual comprehension. They don't really get into teaching awareness.

Results are caused by actions. Actions are caused by the paradigm, by what's going on the person's subconscious mind. The idea in the subconscious mind causes the body to move in action and produce the results it's

---

Nothing goes into the subconscious mind without first going through the conscious mind.

---

getting. The conscious mind is the clearinghouse. Nothing goes to the subconscious without going through the conscious mind.

Why, then, would anyone choose ideas that produce results they don't want? There's one cause: they're not thinking. Ignorance is the problem—also habit, which is nothing but the expression of the paradigm. That's sad, but that's the way it works.

Pay very close attention to this: A person is looking at their results. OK. Those results are there; you can't deny them. The conscious mind is filled with the image of those results. We look at our financial situation and we say, "It's here; you can't deny it. This is what I've got."

This is the way people believe. They believe in the physical, because they're looking at the situation through their senses; they were raised to live through their senses. They get emotionally involved with their situation, and they produce more of the same thing. It's a self-fulfilling cycle of doom. They keep doing the same thing over and over again.

Why won't they change? They don't understand. Do they have dreams? They have them, but the dreams fade. They're not into a plan for executing their dreams.

The starting point here is results. If the starting point is results, they will dictate the thoughts. The thoughts then produce the feelings, the feelings produce the actions, and the actions produce more of the same results. That's a cycle of doom.

The starting point is wrong. Here's where we should see a person thinking *into* results regardless of their present results. This person starts out thinking of what they want. When you think of what you want, you see what you want. That causes feelings, which cause actions, which cause results: you get what you want. You see new, improved results.

That's how you keep winding it up. You see big results. The results cause the thinking, thinking causes feeling, the feelings cause the actions. You produce the results you want, and then you get into thinking bigger and better results.

You'll hear people say, "But you can't ignore the results. You can't ignore the fact there's nothing in the bank account." No, you can't. But you don't have to stand and stare at the damn thing, believing you've got to keep thinking about it. The memory is there. You'll remember it.

You have higher faculties too: perception, will, imagination, intuition, reason. You want to put one or another of these to work. You put the imagination to work. You build a picture of the good that you desire. What do you want? You build that picture in your consciousness; then

Use these higher faculties of your conscious
mind to feed your subconscious mind:
• Perception
• Will
• Imagination
• Intuition
• Reason

you take what you want and you plant that in your heart.
The Bible says that as a person thinks in their heart, so
are they. You now start to get emotionally involved with
what you want. As you start feeding that, there develops a
desire. A desire is the effort of the unexpressed possibility
within seeking expression without through your action.
That changes the vibration. As the vibration changes the
action, the action changes the results, also changing what
you attract.

In short, the first principle is thought. It starts with
the thought, not the results.

Many people believe that success is a matter of being
in the right place at the right time. I think there's a shred
of truth in that, but you've got to be aware that you're
in the right place at the right time. When the dot-coms
were coming out, I had different opportunities. I could
have earned millions, but I wasn't interested in that; it

wasn't what I was doing. What I'm doing isn't just about the money. I want to earn a lot of money, because that enables me to do what I'm doing in a bigger way. Money is the medium that helps us amplify what we're doing. But if I were just doing it for the money, I'd have a lot of money, and that would be it. Is that what this all about? I don't think so. It's about the goal.

Wattles also writes:

> There is no labor from which most people shrink as they do from that of sustained and consecutive thought; it is the hardest work in the world. This is especially true when truth is contrary to appearances. Every appearance in the visible world tends to produce a corresponding form in the mind which observes it; and this can only be prevented by holding the thought of the TRUTH.

You see, if the bank account is empty, it's very hard not to think, "Empty bank account. I've got to earn some money. I need the money." This can only be prevented by holding the thought of the truth and seeing the abundance of what you want.

Wattles continues:

> To look upon the appearance of disease will produce the form of disease in your own mind, and ultimately

in your body, unless you hold the thought of the truth, which is that there is no disease; it is only an appearance, and the reality is health.

To look upon the appearances of poverty will produce corresponding forms in your own mind, unless you hold to the truth that there is no poverty; there is only abundance.

To think health when surrounded by the appearances of disease, or to think riches when in the midst of appearances of poverty, requires power; but he who acquires this power becomes a MASTER MIND. He can conquer fate; he can have what he wants.

You may say, "I don't understand that." You know something? You don't really have to understand it, but you have to believe it.

This power can only be acquired by getting hold of the basic fact which is behind all appearances; and that fact is that there is one Thinking Substance, from which and by which all things are made.

Then we must grasp the truth that every thought held in this substance becomes a form, and that man can so impress his thoughts upon it as to cause them to take form and become visible things.

When we realize this, we lose all doubt and fear, for we know that we can create what we want

> "Man can form things in his thought,
> and by impressing his thought upon
> formless substance, can cause the thing
> he thinks about to be created."
> —Wallace Wattles

to create; we can get what we want to have, and can become what we want to be. As a first step toward getting rich, you must believe the three fundamental statements given previously in this chapter; and in order to emphasize them. I repeat them here:

There is a thinking stuff from which all things are made, and which, in its original state, permeates, penetrates, and fills the interspaces of the universe.

A thought, in this substance, produces the thing that is imaged by the thought.

Man can form things in his thought, and, by impressing his thought upon formless substance, can cause the thing he thinks about to be created.

You must lay aside all other concepts of the universe than this monistic one; and you must dwell upon this until it is fixed in your mind, and has become your habitual thought. Read these creed statements over and over again; fix every word upon your memory, and meditate upon them until you firmly believe what they say. If a doubt comes to you, cast it aside as a sin. Do not listen to arguments against this idea; do not go to churches or lectures where a contrary concept of things is taught or preached. Do not read magazines or books which teach a different idea; if you get mixed up in your faith, all your efforts will be in vain.

Do not ask why these things are true, nor speculate as to how they can be true; simply take them on trust.

The science of getting rich begins with the absolute acceptance of this faith.

All of this may sound pretty strange to you, but I'm going to tell you something: all the people I know that really subscribe to these ideas do a lot of good. They really believe that they are God's greatest form of creation. They're totally locked into a service-oriented life. All they want to do is figure out how to make everything bigger and better—expansion and fuller expression—and they can do it.

Now I want you to take a few minutes to answer the questions below.

What is the first step towards getting rich?

What is mankind, and what power do we have?

What is the basic fact behind all appearance?

What must you do and what must you believe if you are to practice the Science of Getting Rich?

What requires the expenditure of more power than any other work a person has to perform, and why?

Answer these questions. Take the time now to do it.

When you start working with this material, it may feel like drinking from a fire hose. In the five years I was with the fire department, I put out a lot of fires. The water coming out of a fire hose will knock you down. I would imagine that if somebody tried to drink out of one, it would be quite wild. These ideas can be overwhelming. If you feel lost, that's OK. Don't let that bother you. We're going into some pretty big ideas here. Don't feel bad if they overwhelm you. Don't feel bad if you say, "I don't think I can do this." Yes, you can. You're already doing it. You're already thinking. You've got mental activity going on. It's just a matter of doing it right.

If I were to look in your bank account or your life, I would be able to tell you exactly what's going on. As a matter of fact, if you've been in a seminar that I've taught or have been physically in a room with me, you would know that I can walk up to a person and tell exactly what's going on in their mind. That's because everything going on the inside shows on the outside. I can read it. I can feel it. I have a very highly tuned intuitive factor. My psyche is really sharp, because I study this material all the time; I'm forever sharpening my abilities.

Anyone doing anything over a period of time is going to get better at it. You will get better at studying this. Don't let it overwhelm you. Don't be at all ashamed to say, "I'm having trouble." Everybody has trouble. You're making an enormous switch in your life.

Keep this in mind: only about 3–5 percent of people (I'm being very generous here) would really understand these ideas and use them every day. The other 95 percent of the population—they don't get it. To that 95 percent, this sounds preposterous; it doesn't make any sense at all.

You can get really good at this process. But if you're a little overwhelmed and you're thinking, "I'm not going to be able to take all this in," just kept reading and studying over the next year. If you feel you're getting behind, forget it: you're not. Just let the past go.

Wattles writes, "To look upon the appearances of poverty will produce corresponding forms in your own mind, unless you hold to the truth that there is no poverty; there is only abundance."

I went to the extent of cutting pieces of paper to the same size as money. I would take a couple of $100 bills and put them on the outside. I actually only had $200, but it would look as if I had $2,200. I would carry that in my pocket.

If you develop a good rapport with money, you will begin to attract it. I attract a lot of money, and I give a lot away. That's another part of the secret: to give. You willingly give and graciously receive, and you can't give too much. The more you learn that, the better off you're going to be. When I first started, I didn't know how to receive. A mentor of mine said, "Then you haven't learned how to give."

"What are you talking about?"

"Giving and receiving are the same thing, Bob."

I have a friend out on the West Coast, Jane Willhite, who owns PSI World, which teaches techniques for gaining power, freedom, and happiness in life. She says, "Givers gain," and I love that.

We're talking about levels of awareness. You start out on the bottom in an animalistic state, as a little baby. The baby reacts to everything that's happening. When you learn mastery, you don't react. You respond. When you're react, it's fight or flight. That's where animals live. They react to what's going on. The people that master these teachings don't react to anything, they respond. They think and plan.

It is said, "Observation is power. Judgment is weakness." That's a very powerful statement. When anything happens, you observe it. Let's suppose a person is not treating you very nicely. Are you going to react? If you're tired and not very aware, you probably will react, and it's fight or flight. It's not a good place to live. Otherwise you would ask yourself, "I wonder why they're doing that. Why would they be that way? They must be very unhappy."

When we're born, we're down at the bottom in an animalistic state; that's where we are. Next we go into mass consciousness. The kid gets a little older and goes outside to be like the rest of the kids. Isn't that what kids do? They follow the masses. They want to dress the same. If somebody's got those new running shoes, they want those new running shoes.

It's mass consciousness. They all go the same way together. "Well, they can't all be wrong." Listen, here's a rule: if you're going to follow other people, and you see a large mass of people going one way and one or two going the other way, follow the one or two. Historically, the masses have always been going in the wrong direction.

Eventually something happens inside, and you move ahead. A person aspires to do something greater. It might be positive, it might be negative, but there's an aspiration. You want to do something bigger, although you don't know what it is.

> "Observation is power.
> Judgment is weakness."

I'll tell you exactly what it is. It's the higher side of your personality, your uniqueness, wanting to be expressed. You see, there's something inside of you: your spiritual DNA. Perfection is within you. That perfection seeks to express itself within and through you, because spirit is always for expansion and fuller expression, never for disintegration.

I remember when this happened to me. I had a desire for something greater than I had. I didn't know what it was, but I wanted more. The feeling came from reading Wattles' and other books and listening to audio recordings. I just kept reading and listening to them. God, I was having a hell of a time. I had a paradigm that would blow you away; it was terrible. But I had this desire, and the desire kept growing. I'd want to go ahead. I had this unique feeling that I wanted to do something, but the masses would pull me back. When this desire got going, bang, I would be pulled back again.

If you're experiencing that, understand what's happening. You're breaking away from the old conditioned you. That conditioning is strong; it's in every molecule of your being. It may date back generations. Your genetic conditioning goes back for generations. A little particle of energy from mom and another little part from dad came swinging along and bang! They were in resonance. That was the start of you. Over 280 days, it kept attracting more of the same kind of energy. What was mom's particle of energy? Where did mom come from? She came from her mom and dad. Where dad come from? From his mom and dad. These little particles of energy go back for generations as genetic structuring; God knows how far.

Then, 280 days later, you make your debut in the planet. Your mind is like an open cup. Whatever's going on around goes right into the subconscious mind. That's how the paradigm and the conditioning are formed. This is what you're breaking out of.

You've got a unique feeling inside, a strong desire. Wattles said that desire is the effort of the unexpressed possibility within seeking expression without through your action. Every time you go for it, the paradigm pulls your back. There's a war going on in our mind.

Once you get to this point, you might as well keep going, because if you don't, the war will continue. It will get worse, because this desire is not going to leave you. You've stirred something up; you've caused it to happen inside of yourself. If you don't know what's happening, the odds are, you're going to have one hell of a time. If you do know, you're still going to have a hell of a time, but at least you know what's going on, so you can work your way out of it.

Then one day you realize, "Discipline: that's what I need. I've got to give myself a command, and I'm going to follow it." You go for it, and you discipline yourself.

All of a sudden, that discipline starts to fade. You think, "Oh, hell, it was nothing but a wish. It didn't change at all." The confusion is still there, and you realize you're stuck. That's a terrible place to be.

If you're stuck, stay with your goal anyway. Discipline is the key—the ability to give yourself a command and follow it. If you really want something but you don't couple it with discipline, you're screwed. It isn't going to happen. Wish and discipline need to be inseparably attached.

You discipline yourself. As soon as your wish starts to fade, you say, "That's it. I am not letting that happen. I am going to discipline myself. I'm going to ride this thing out. I don't give a damn if I'm confused. I don't care if I'm overwhelmed. I will stick with this, and I'm going to make it work."

Here's what happens next. You get hit with a new idea. You move it into action. The actions change the results, and all of this starts to change. Just watch it. When it happens, it is the nicest thing. It's very subtle. You have mastered the concept of controlling your own thinking. You don't react anymore. You think, "I know where I'm going, and I know what I'm going to do. She may not want to come with me, he may not want to come with me, but I'm going. Nothing is going to hold me back. I've got a dream"—like Martin Luther King. You've got to have a dream. Then you've got to make sure that you're going for it.

"Desire is the effort of the unexpressed possibility within, seeking expression without, through your action."
—Wallace Wattles

Chapter Four

Increasing Life

In chapter 5 of *The Science of Getting Rich*, Wattles writes: "You must get rid of the last vestige of the old idea that there is a Deity whose will it is that you should be poor, or whose purpose may be served by keeping you in poverty." God loves you and wants you to live an abundant life. God offers abundance, greater good, expansion, fuller expression.

"The Intelligent Substance which is All, and in All, and which lives in All and lives in you, is a consciously Living Substance," he adds. The power that's causing the plants, trees and everything to grow flows to and through you. "Being a consciously living substance, It must have the nature and inherent desire of every living intelligence for increase of life. Every living thing must continually seek for the enlargement of its life, because life, in the mere act of living, must increase itself."

You see it in every form of life. When you look at all of nature, you see expansion and expression. The only place where it is not properly expressed is where people are in charge.

Where I live, we have a big vine on the fence on the west side of our house, a magnificent vine. It's a beautiful vine. It covers the whole fence.

A year or two ago, we decided we were going to replace the fence, because it was starting to get decrepit. I thought about it for a long time, because I thought we'd have to get rid of the vine. They took the fence down and put a new one up, and fortunately the vine stayed. It's so beautiful. That's life, expressing itself in a greater way.

"A seed, dropped into the ground, springs into activity," Wattles writes, "and in the act of living produces a hundred more seeds; life, by living, multiplies itself. It is forever Becoming More; it must do so, if it continues to be at all."

Inspirational leader Robert Schuller said, "Anyone can tell how many seeds are in an apple. But no one can tell how many apples are in a seed." That's essentially what this passage is saying.

To continue to exist, you've got to grow. If you don't, you're going to die; in fact, that's what dying is all about. I think retirement is the most despicable concept anybody ever originated. Why would anybody think of it?

> "Anyone call tell how many seeds are
> in an apple. But, no one can tell
> how many apples are in a seed."
> —Robert Schuller

Years ago, when I was a fireman, we used to sit around the fire halls, and all the guys could talk about was when they could retire. They were always trying to get the union to lower the retirement age. I started reading this book sitting in the fire hall. What I was hearing and what I was reading were polar opposites. I thought, "Why would anybody want to retire? There's no way I want to retire." To continue with Wattles:

> Intelligence is under this same necessity for continuous increase. Every thought we think makes it necessary for us to think another thought; consciousness is continually expanding. Every fact we learn leads us to the learning of another fact; knowledge is continually increasing. Every talent we cultivate brings to the mind the desire to cultivate another talent; we are subject to the urge of life, seeking expression, which ever drives us on to know more, to do more, and to be more.

There's a great lesson that ties in with this: *Your imagination is either keeping you stuck or leading you to new terri-*

tory. How are you using yours? Life and spirit are flowing through you, and, again, spirit is always for expansion and fuller expression. We have urges to grow. If you start suppressing them, you're going to have trouble in your physical body.

"In order to know more, do more, and be more," Wattles tells us, "we must have more; we must have things to use, for we learn, and do, and become, only by using things. We must get rich, so that we can live more." You don't acquire riches just to pile up a bunch of money in bank account or something like that. Riches are to help you use more of life.

Money is the medium of exchange we use for another person's product or service. We didn't always have money. If you go back far enough, it was all a barter system. If you go back still further, I might say, "Listen, I don't like hunting."

Someone else says, "If you make my arrows for me, I'll do your hunting for you."

Another person asks, "How come you don't have to make any arrows?"

"I have somebody else who makes them for me. I do their hunting for them. They make good arrows; they're really straight, and you really hunt well with them."

The other guy says, "I wonder if they'd make them for me."

"I don't know. Go and ask them."

The third guy goes and asks me, but I say, "No, I don't need any more meat. I'm already getting me enough."

This is where money comes in. We have to have something to use as a medium of exchange for the product or services of other people.

> The desire for riches is simply the capacity for larger life seeking fulfillment; every desire is the effort of an unexpressed possibility to come into action. It is power seeking to manifest which causes desire. That which makes you want more money is the same as that which makes the plant grow; it is Life, seeking fuller expression.

Desire is the idea in the subconscious mind that wants to express itself in a greater way. That which makes you want more money is the same as that which makes the plant grow. It is life seeking fuller expression. The essence of life in the center of your consciousness is perfection seeking expression within and through you.

Now here's our problem. We sit and think, "I would like to have this, but I can't have it." The very fact that you even thought about it is proof that you can have it, although you may not know how to get it. You can have whatever you want.

Here's the trick. When you're going after a goal, if you know how to get it, you're going sideways: you're doing something you already know how to do. You want to set a goal that causes you to go where you've never been. Sir Edmund Hillary didn't know how to get to the top of Mount Everest until after he got there. The Wright brothers didn't know how to get the plane off the ground until after they got in the air.

> It is the desire of God that you should get rich. He wants you to get rich because he can express himself better through you if you have plenty of things to use in giving him expression. He can live more in you if you have unlimited command of the means of life.

You're not God. You're an expression of God. You're here to do God's work. God wants to do greater good than has been done within and through you. That's why you have the desire for more, to do more, to be more. As you do those things, you've got to grow; you've got to become a bigger person and become more aware. What do we become more aware of? We become more aware of our oneness with God. We become more aware of our oneness with this infinite power, which operates in an orderly way. We become more aware of the mental faculties that we've got and how to utilize them properly. It's all in awareness.

I make all my own PowerPoint slides. I had tremendous difficulty in learning how; there's so much informa-

> "You want to set a goal that causes you
> to go where you've never been. Sir Edmund
> Hillary didn't' know how to get to the top
> of Mount Everest until after he got there."
> —Bob Proctor

tion to acquire. But I did learn, and I learned many other things in the process. This too is spirit expressing itself. You want to do something; you want to learn. Don't look at learning something as a bad thing. It's a good thing. It's causing you to become more aware. Now I'm more aware of how to make slides than I was before. That's how we learn. We're developing our greater awareness.

The universe desires you to have everything you want to have.

Nature is friendly to your plans.

Everything is naturally for you.

Make up your mind that this is true.

It is essential, however that *your purpose should harmonize with the purpose that is in All.*

You've got to have a purpose in life. I have a purpose. My purpose is to live and work in an environment that's conducive to my unfoldment so that I can serve more—I can serve my family, my company, my community, my nation, and ultimately the world in new and greater ways. We've got to have this purpose: it's all to make things better.

> You must want real life, not mere pleasure or sensual gratification. Life is the performance of function; and the individual really lives only when he performs every function, physical, mental, and spiritual, of which he is capable, without excess in any.
>
> You do not want to get rich in order to live swinishly, for the gratification of animal desires; that is not life. But the performance of every physical function is a part of life, and no one lives completely who denies the impulses of the body a normal and healthful expression.
>
> You do not want to get rich solely to enjoy mental pleasures, to get knowledge, to gratify ambition, to outshine others, to be famous. All these are a legitimate parts of life, but the man who lives for the pleasures of the intellect alone will only have a partial life, and he will never be satisfied with his lot.

Napoleon Hill wrote, "An educated person is a person who has so developed the faculties of their mind that they may acquire anything they want, or its equivalent, without violating the rights of others."

"An educated person is a person who has so developed the faculties of their mind that they may acquire anything they want, or its equivalent, without violating the rights of others."
—Napoleon Hill

Now I can ask you: could you write down what the faculties of your mind are? Don't feel bad if you can't, because ninety-eight out of a hundred people cannot tell you what the faculties of the mind are.

We have physical faculties: we can see, hear, smell, taste, and touch. When you are put under anesthetic, they're suppressing your sensory factors. You're not conscious of what's going on. Your sensory factors are strictly for your physical benefit. They help you correspond and communicate with the outside world.

But if you're going to go beyond the physical, if you're going to deal with the nonphysical world, if you're going to get into mind development and understand the spiritual side of your personality, you must understand your higher faculties.

Your spiritual DNA is perfect. It requires no modification or improvement. Spirit is all-knowing, it's all-powerful, and it's ever present. All the knowledge there ever was or ever will be is in spirit. All the power there ever was or ever will be is in spirit. Spirit is omnipresent. It's everywhere at the same time.

Do you know what that means? That means it's within me. They didn't say that spirit was present everywhere except in Bob. It's ever present, 100 percent, evenly present all at the same time.

That is the real you. You are the offspring of a deathless soul. You are God's creation. God created you in God's image.

Here's the problem. We're created in God's image, but we don't understand that. Actually, we've really messed it up, because we've created God in our image. We see God as a man, in one place.

How could that man have all knowledge and all power and be evenly present in all places at the same time? We don't know how to answer that. We say, "We're not supposed to know those things." That's how you get off the hook.

The truth is, you're talking about a God that's 100 percent evenly present, in all places at the same time. It's all-knowing, with all the knowledge there ever was or ever will be. Look at your smartphone. The way to make one of these has always been here. It just took a few people to wake up and expand the mind, and suddenly we all have smartphones. There's more power in one of these little handheld pocket computers than there was in the computer that took the first rocket to the moon.

This gives you an idea of where we're going. Spirit is all-powerful. That's you. You have all the power within you. All the knowledge is within you—everything you need.

How do we have access to that? As we've seen, the mind is divided into two parts: the conscious and the subconscious. The conscious mind is hooked up to sensory factors, which are like little antennae that help us correspond and communicate with the outside world.

The conscious mind is also the intellectual mind. The intellectual mind dictates how we use our emotions. The emotions express themselves through the body: we call that *vibration*. The emotion is the vibration.

How do we control the vibration? Through the intellectual factors—perception, will, imagination, memory, intuition, and reason. The sad part is, we're taught nothing about this in school. We've got all these faculties from the time we were little kids, but we don't use them. Yet they are all here in our conscious mind, and they are powerful.

Power flows into consciousness through the use of the imagination: we build ideas. The idea is to plant those ideas in the heart: "As he thinketh in his heart, so

---

We control the vibration of emotions through six intellectual factors: perception, will, imagination, memory, intuition and reason.

---

is he" (Proverbs 23:7). We build the picture, and we plant it in the heart.

How do we build the picture? It starts with spirit, which gives us the want. It's the want inside that wishes to express itself in a greater way. From the inside, we want. If you ask somebody, "Why do you want it?" they don't really know. Little kids are asked, "Why do you want that?" The kid doesn't know. The kid wants it because spirit is causing them to want it; spirit wants to express itself through them.

When the want comes into our consciousness, we use our imagination to turn the want into something we can see and talk about. Then we take that want, and we give it back to spirit. We put it back into the heart. The heart is the divine center of your life: the heart encompasses all of you. The heart, the spirit in you, feeds into your consciousness, causing you to consciously want something. When the want comes, you use your imagination to expand what you want and make it crystal clear; then you plant that want in your heart. By planting it in your heart, using repetition, it turns into a desire, which alters the vibration, which changes the results. As you start dealing with your higher faculties, you're getting into your genius, which is within every one of us.

If I'm coaching a person, I'll say, "Tell me exactly what you want." Most people won't do that. They're shy. They hold their desires inside: "What would you think of

> "2 percent of the people think, 3 percent of the people think they think, and 95 percent of the people would rather die than think."
> —Dr. Kenneth McFarland

me if I told you what I wanted?" What you tell me isn't going to change my opinion of you at all. I've already got an opinion of you: I see you as absolute genius. Are you expressing it? Are you bringing it out? Is there a free flow? In most people, there isn't. When I sit down with somebody, I want to know exactly what they want. How do you really want to live?

You begin by using your higher faculties. You unlock the powers of your mind. Your inductive, reasoning factor gives you the ability to tap into pure unadulterated spirit. You can think. You can do it underwater, in a plane, in the bathtub, walking down the street—wherever you are. You thereby tap into spirit, and you can pluck out little parts, pull them all together, and build ideas. That's what the inductive, reasoning factor does. That is called the *thinker*. Most people never truly develop it.

Henry Ford said that thinking is the hardest work there is, which is probably why so few people engage in it. Educator Dr. Kenneth McFarland said that 2 percent of the people think, 3 percent of the people think they think, and 95 percent would rather die than think. I'm inclined to agree with him. If you believe everybody thinks, listen to what's going on around you. It's obvious that they're not thinking.

I hear people talking about the most terrible things. I ask, "Why are you thinking about that? Why are you even going there? Don't you understand that whatever you're thinking about, you're becoming? You're in harmony with it; you're going to attract it to you. Think about the good things. Think about the dynamo that you are. Think about the phenomenal power that's flowing to and through you. Think. Really think."

Let's turn to perception. I've already quoted Dr. Wayne Dyer: "When you change the way you look at something, the thing you're looking at changes."

Every now and then, if I have a problem and I'm having difficulty solving it, I write the problem out in as much detail as I can, in the present tense. Then I put the problem in the center of my desk or possibly the dining room table, I sit down in a chair, and I look at it. I say, "Is that problem in me, or is it on the paper?" It may take me a while, but I've got to get that problem out of me and onto the paper. That is the only way I'm going to become objective.

Then I'll ask, "How would Napoleon Hill look at this?" Then I may go, sit at another side of the table, and ask, "How would Earl Nightingale look at this?" I may go to the end of the table and ask, "How would Henry Ford look at this?"

You can get into the spirit of Ford; you can get in the spirit of Hill or Nightingale; you can get into the spirit of those people and look at your problem from their perspective. You're going to get many different points of view.

Pretty soon, your perception is going to shift dramatically. You may find that a big problem isn't such a big problem after all.

Let's go into intuition. Your intuition is a mental faculty that enables you to pick up vibration and translate it in your brain. Sometimes you're not able to translate it, but you can pick it up.

When you meet another person, that person has massive energy, and they express what's going on in their mind through vibration; they express their thoughts, feelings, and actions in vibration. Your intuitive factor can pick up that energy.

I don't care if you think you've got a highly evolved intuitive factor or not; when you are with people, you pick up their mood. Something's obviously bothering them, and you wonder what it is. Your intuitive factor picked up that energy and is telling you something is bothering them.

I can walk up to you in a seminar, and I can read your energy like a book. Every now and then I do that just to show people I can do it. If I can, you can. Whenever you see one person doing something, that's proof it can be done. You have the same abilities they have; you can do what they do. We're all psychic—every one of us.

Your intuitive factor picks up vibration, and you have messages coming at you all the time. You may be thinking about someone you haven't talked to for a long time. Then the phone rings, and it's that person on the phone. You say, "What a coincidence! I was just thinking of you." It's not a coincidence at all. It's thought transference, and it goes on all the time. It's your intuitive factor that picks it up.

How do you develop your intuition? When you're with another person, all of your conscious attention has to be on that person. That's not the way most people operate. Most people place their conscious attention on themselves. They are hoping their tie is straight, they're afraid they've got food on their face, or they're wondering what the other person is thinking of them. You've got to get rid of that nonsense. Quit worrying about what people think of you. If you knew how little they thought about you, you wouldn't be worried about what they're thinking.

Take all of your consciousness and put it on the other person. Really focus. Listen. Actively listen to the person. Hear everything they're saying. Really pay attention, and don't get so excited about answering them that you interrupt them. Listen until they're finished. That way you'll start developing your intuition; you really will. Intuition.

"Quit worrying what people think of you. If you knew how little they thought about you, you wouldn't be worried what they're thinking."
—Bob Proctor

Memory is another mental faculty. One time I brought memory expert Harry Lorayne to a meeting in Toronto. It's an hour flight to Toronto from New York City. Harry got a copy of *Newsweek* or *Time* and memorized the whole magazine on the way to Toronto on the plane.

When Harry got here, he had his assistant make copies of each page. We had 3,000 people come into the convention center, and we handed out hundreds of these pages. Harry stood by one door, meeting people.

When Harry got up on the stage, he said, "If I met you when you came in, stand up." A large number of people stood up. He started to tell every one of them their names. If the name was hard to pronounce, he spelled it. Then he had people reading from the pages at random. They'd stop, and he would continue on reciting from where they stopped. He told them exactly what advertisement was on each page. He blew people's minds.

There's no end to our memory. We have perfect memory. These mental muscles can be developed to a phenomenal degree, but they need exercise. If every day I lifted weights with one arm and left the other in a sling, pretty soon one arm would have very powerful muscles, and the other would be rendered useless. It's the same with the mind. What you don't use, you lose, and what you exercise becomes stronger.

The will is yet another mental faculty. It enables you to hold one idea on the screen of the mind to the exclusion of all others. Remember, we've got five senses operating like little antennae. They're picking up all kinds of noise that's going on outside—a siren, a fire truck, a police car, a construction site. You can shut all that down and bring all of your conscious attention to focus on one idea—through the will.

Power flows to and through us. When the power comes into us, it has no form. It's pure unadulterated creative spirit. We give it form, and then we send it back out through the universe. You can increase the amplitude of vibration, making it much more powerful through concentration.

If you don't think there's power in concentration, think of this: You could be shopping in a mall, and all of a sudden you feel uncomfortable. You feel somebody behind you staring at you, you turn around quickly, and sure enough, there's somebody staring. They look away and they start walking away. When they're staring at

---

The subconscious mind will accept whatever you plant in it. That's why it's so important to plant good things.

---

you, they're concentrating on you. They're sending off a powerful charge of energy that's causing you to feel it.

Concentration increases amplitude of vibration. It strengthens the power leaving you. Someone asks can you shorten the time it takes you to reach your goal. Yes—through concentration. Concentration increases amplitude of vibration. The more energy you give to the goal, the shorter the span of incubation. We've got to give more energy to our goal, and we do that through the will to concentrate. As von Braun told Kennedy, all it would take to reach the moon was the will to do it.

The imagination is such a marvelous tool. Everything that is made is first made in the imagination. When you imagine something and turn it over to your subconscious mind, the subconscious cannot tell whether it's real. As we've seen, the subconscious mind is amoral. Like the earth, it doesn't care what you plant, but it will return what you plant. Similarly, the subconscious mind will accept whatever you plant in it. That's why it's so important to imagine good things. You build a beautiful idea.

We are all geniuses, but you get into your genius by developing these higher faculties. Spirit is omnipresent. Thoughts are omnipresent. You choose the ones you want, you pull those together, and you build an idea. When idea is built, you hold on to it, because it's what you want. That's how you set your goal.

Chapter Five

How Riches Come to You

Let me begin this chapter with a quotation from "The Big Money," by Napoleon Hill.

When money comes in quantities known as "the big money," it flows to the one who accumulates it, as easily as water flows down hill. There exists a great unseen stream of POWER, which may be compared to a river; except that one side flows in one direction, carrying all who get into that side of the stream, onward and upward to WEALTH—and the other side flows in the opposite direction, carrying all who are unfortunate enough to get into it (and not able to extricate themselves from it), downward to misery and POVERTY.

"When riches take the place of poverty,
the change is usually brought about through
well-conceived and carefully executed PLANS.
Poverty needs no plan."
—Napoleon Hill

Every man who has accumulated a great fortune, has recognized the existence of this stream of life. It consists of one's THINKING PROCESS. The positive emotions of thought form the side of the stream which carries one to fortune. The negative emotions form the side which carries one down to poverty.

This carries a thought of stupendous importance to the person who is following this with the object of accumulating a fortune. If you are in the side of the stream of POWER which leads to poverty, this may serve as an oar, by which you may propel yourself over into the other side of the stream. It can serve you ONLY through application and use. Merely reading, and passing judgment on it, either one way or another, will in no way benefit you.

Poverty and riches often change places. Poverty may, and generally does, voluntarily take the place of riches. When riches take the place of poverty, the change is usually brought about through well-conceived and carefully executed PLANS. Poverty needs no plan. It needs no one to aid it, because it is bold and ruthless. Riches are shy and timid. They have to be "attracted."

In chapter 6 of *The Science of Getting Rich*, Wattles writes:

When I say that you do not have to drive sharp bargains, I do not mean that you do not have to drive any bargains at all, or that you are above the necessity for having any dealings with your fellow men. I mean that you will not need to deal with them unfairly; you do not have to get something for nothing, *but can give to every man more than you take from him.*

You cannot give every man more in cash market value than you take from him, but you can give him more in use value than the cash value of the thing you take from him. The paper, ink, and other material in this book may not be worth the money you pay for it; but if the ideas suggested by it bring you thousands of dollars, you have not been wronged by those who sold it to you; they have given you a great use value for a small cash value.

Let us suppose that I own a picture by one of the great artists, which, in any civilized community, is worth thousands of dollars. I take it to Baffin Bay, and by "salesmanship" induce an Eskimo to give a bundle of furs worth $500 for it. I have really wronged him, for he has no use for the picture; it has no use value to him; it will not *add to his life.*

But suppose I give him a gun worth $50 for his furs; then he has made a good bargain. He has use for the gun; it will get him many more furs and much food; it will add to his life in every way; it will make him rich.

When you rise from the competitive to the creative plane, you can scan your business transactions very strictly, and if you are selling any man anything which does not add more to his life than the thing he gives you in exchange, you can afford to stop it. You do not have to beat anybody in business. And if you are in a business which does beat people, get out of it at once.

Give every man more in use value than you take from him in cash value; then you are adding to the life of the world by every business transaction.

A lot of people talk about their piece of the pie, and it gets to a point where they think, "If I want more pie, I've got to take somebody else's pie." That's not the way it is at all. The trick is to make a bigger pie, so everybody can have more.

The law of compensation states that the amount of money you earn will always be in exact ratio to the need for what you do, your ability to do it, and the difficulty of replacing you. Of those three steps, there's only one that you have to focus on: your ability to do it. You want to become a master of whatever you do.

So you want to ask yourself, how good am I at doing what I'm doing?

Everybody wants freedom—time and money freedom. And you're going to be amazed how much free time you have when you never have to think about money. I can remember when I had to think about money all the time, because I owed money to everybody and his brother. In that situation money dominates your thinking, because your creditors aren't going to let you go.

> The law of compensation states that the amount of money your earn is composed of three factors:
> 1. The need for what you do.
> 2. Your ability to do it.
> 3. The difficulty of replacing you.

They're going to call you, asking, "Where's the money?" If you want free time, clean up any money situation that you've got; get rid of it.

When you never have to think about money, it's amazing how much free time you have. Now I spend almost all my time brainstorming with brilliant people about how many millions we could earn. Then we switch over to the cause. If you want to earn $10 million, you've got to provide $10 million worth of service. So how can I provide $10 million of service? You don't have to provide it all to one person; it could be all over the place.

In the quote at the beginning of this chapter, Napoleon Hill said that money is like a river, and it is. One side goes onward to wealth and prosperity, and the other side goes in the other direction, to poverty, to lack and limitation. Get into the habit of going after the big money.

There are only three strategies for earning money. Although there are a million different places you can go to employ three strategies, there are still only three: M1, M2 and M3. Now I was taught virtually nothing about earning money when I was a kid. I learned nothing about earning money in school; there was no talk about it at all. When I left school and got jobs, nobody talked about money. I knew nothing about earning money, so I always worked using M1, the small strategy. I stumbled on the M3 strategy by accident. I didn't really understand what

> Three strategies for earning money:
> 1. M1: Trading your time for money. (96 percent of the population)
> 2. M2: Investing your money to earn money. (3 percent of the population)
> 3. M3: Multiple sources of income; multiplied from the efforts of others. (1 percent of the population)

happened; I started to multiply my income without really knowing what I was doing.

M1 is where almost all people are. In fact, 96 percent of the people follow the M1 strategy. It's not a good one. That's where people trade their time for money. I don't care how much you get an hour: if you're working by the hour, you're doing it the wrong way. Charge by the job; don't charge by the hour.

M2 is an excellent strategy. It's only used by 3 percent of the population, just three people in a hundred, and for a very good reason. That's where you invest money to earn money. Most people don't have any money to invest; that's why only 3 percent are involved in this approach.

M3 is used by 1 percent of people. It's something I stumbled on back in the sixties. I had absolutely no idea what I was doing, but, even though I had no formal education or business experience, my income went from \$4,000 a year to \$14,500 a month in one year. If you annualize \$14,500 a month, you're talking about \$175,000 a year. When you go from \$4,000 to \$175,000 in a year, something very dramatic has happened.

It took me quite a few years to figure out what happened. How come I'm earning so much money? I was raised to believe that if you're going to earn a lot of money, you've got to be really smart. I knew I wasn't that smart. You don't have to be very smart. You've just got to be on the right side of the river. This is where you multiply your time through the efforts of others, you set up multiple sources of income, and you multiply your time. Anybody can utilize this idea. Do all of these sources of income have to be the same size? No. Some can be big, some can be small, and some won't work out at all; you keep improving what you're doing.

Wattles goes on to write:

Finally, because you are to cause the creation of your riches from Formless Substance which permeates all your environment, it does not follow that they are to take shape from the atmosphere and come into being before your eyes.

If you want a sewing machine, for instance, I do not mean to tell you that you are to impress the thought of a sewing machine on Thinking Substance until the machine is formed without hands, in the room where you sit, or elsewhere. But if you want a sewing machine, hold the mental image of it with the most positive certainty that it is being made, or is on its way to you. After once forming the thought, have the most absolute and unquestioning faith that the sewing machine is coming; never think of it, or speak, of it, in any other way than as being sure to arrive. Claim it as already yours.

In short, you've got to get a picture of what you're asking spirit for. The picture has to be very clear. Then you've got to impress that upon what Wattles calls "the Thinking Substance." The picture you plant is exactly what's going to come to you, because as you plant the picture, you control the vibration that you're in, which dictates what you attract to you.

Napoleon Hill puts it beautifully: "The imagination is the most marvelous, miraculous, inconceivably powerful force the world has ever known." Another great teacher of mind control—Neville Goddard, who usually just went by the name "Neville"—writes in his book *The Power of Awareness and Awakened Imagination*: "You must imagine yourself right into the state of your fulfilled desire. This is not mere fancy but a truth you can prove by experience."

You enter into the wish fulfilled. That is called *thinking from the end*. Neville said, "It's overpoweringly real when you think from it." We don't want to just think of something as if it's outside of ourselves, something that we don't have. We want to think from the place where we already have it, and then it becomes real. As Neville says, "Determined imagination, thinking from the end, is the beginning of all miracles. The future must become the present in the imagination of the one who would wisely and consciously create circumstances."

We are creating circumstances, so we've got to be coming from that place. The future is now the present in our imagination.

We're not trying to figure out how to get there. We *are* there. We are experiencing. As Neville states, "We must translate vision into Being. Thinking of into thinking *from*. Imagination must center itself in some state and view the world *from* that state. Thinking *from* the end is an intense perception of the world of fulfilled desire. Thinking *from* the state desired is creative living. Ignorance of this ability to think *from* the end is bondage. It is the root of all bondage with which man is bound. To passively surrender to the evidence of the senses, [to what we're seeing in our physical world, ignoring the whole nonphysical world that we can tap into] underestimates the capacities of the Inner Self. Once man accepts thinking *from* the end as a creative principle in which he can cooperate, then he is redeemed from the absurdity of

"Determined imagination, thinking *from*
the end, is the beginning of all miracles."
—Neville Goddard

ever attempting to achieve his objective by merely thinking *of* it.

When we use our imagination, our objective is not to
think of something outside of ourselves. Our objective is
to feel it as real.

Think of it this way: We live in a spiritual world. We
are spiritual beings. We are living in a physical body. We're
having a physical experience. We have an intellect that
taps us into the spiritual, nonphysical world. In this world
are thoughts. *Thought* and *spirit* are synonymous. We can
tap into this nonphysical world and choose any idea we
want. We choose any thoughts that we want, create an
idea, and hold that idea in our mind. As Earl Nightingale said, "This great dream, this surging dynamic thing
invisible to all the world except to the person who holds
it, is responsible for every great advance of mankind."

You have a big, beautiful dream in your mind. Then
you turn it into a goal. How? You start out with imagination. This is fantasy land. You're dreaming about what
is possible and what you want for yourself.

At this point, you've latched on to something you
want, but it's just a theory. You've got to turn it into a

goal, and you do that by asking yourself two questions: *am I willing?* and *am I able?* Everything we've been discussing tells us absolutely that you are able. You wouldn't love something, you wouldn't want it, if you weren't able to attain it. If you can latch on to that truth and continually become more aware of who you are and the infinite potential within you, you can answer that question very easily. *Yes, I am able.*

Then you have to answer the question, *am I willing?* Am I willing to do what it takes to achieve this goal? This technique, which is called *visioneering*, enables you to lock in at a subconscious level to the idea that you want. It gives you a technique for changing your paradigm. When you link your thought with purpose, you can create amazing things in your life. Visioneering is where you truly begin to create your world through the effective use of your higher faculties. You create and hold the image of what you want.

Your mind, the higher side of your personality, is the much bigger part of yourself. Your physical being is a tiny bit of who you are. Your mind has two distinct parts. Your conscious mind is where you originate ideas as well as where you can accept or reject them. Your subconscious mind is completely different: it cannot tell the difference between what's real and imagined. It must accept everything you give it. What are you giving it?

The conscious mind is also the intellectual mind. That's where your higher faculties are. We're tapping into our higher faculties. We want to use our higher faculties— perception, will, reason, imagination, intuition, memory— to change the paradigm, to create a new paradigm.

With visioneering, we focus on two of them: the imagination and the will. We use them to tap into the nonphysical world, we create an image, and we change our vibration, because we have changed our paradigm. Our paradigm dictates the vibration we're in. It sets up the law of attraction, attracting what's in harmony with us. It's an incredibly powerful tool.

"*Visioneering:* Using the imagination and the will to tap into the nonphysical world, create an image, change your vibration, and attract what you want." —Sandy Gallagher

---

I recommend that you do this practice every day, first thing in the morning, last thing at night. I do it all throughout the day. Once you get really good at this, even just a minute is powerful. It's like turning a light switch on. You feel the shift in your vibration. That's when you know you're doing it right.

To begin with, we shut down our senses. Then we're going to create our want. We're going to bring what we want to the screen of our mind. We are going to create a big, beautiful picture of what we want; we're going to let our imagination fly, so that our want becomes a burning desire. It doesn't matter what anybody else thinks. It doesn't matter what your paradigm thinks. It doesn't matter if your paradigm thinks this is crazy.

As Genevieve Behrend put it, "Train yourself in the practice of deliberately picturing your desire, and carefully examine the picture." Ask yourself, do you have a really clear picture of what you want? Is it a beautiful picture on the screen of your mind? Have you examined the picture to see if it contains all the elements that are important to you? When you turn that picture over to this side of your mind, you start to get emotionally involved. If it's not clear here, it won't be clear in the manifestation.

When you do this practice, you will soon find that your thoughts and your desires proceed in a more orderly procession than ever before. You're moving forward by law. You're moving towards the good that you desire, and it is moving towards you. You're attracting it, and you are moving into action.

When you do this practice, you are aligning your thoughts and desires. You are creating harmony between your conscious mind, your subconscious mind, and your body. You have congruency. You have changed the paradigm so that you're totally in harmony with the good you desire.

"Having reached a state of ordered mentality, you are no longer in a constant state of mental hurry. Hurry is fear and consequently destructive." You have reached a state of ordered mentality. You have clarity in your mind about what you want. You've changed your paradigm. You are experiencing more joy, more beauty, more expansion in your life.

Before you get there, you will go through a phase where it's not all perfect order; you have a difference between what's in your conscious mind and what's in your subconscious mind. But the moment your belief matches with your state, you fuse with it. You're on a higher frequency. You're attracting a whole different caliber of thought. You've elevated your consciousness. As Neville puts it, "It becomes the home from which you view the world. It's your workshop. If you're observant, you will see the outer reality shaping itself upon the model of your imagination."

The subconscious mind just takes what you give it and moves it into action. It does not change anything, it changes nothing. Like the earth, it will grow what you plant in it.

Wattles writes:

Do not forget for a moment that the Thinking Substance is through all, in all, communicating with all, and can influence all. The desire of Thinking Substance for fuller life and better living has caused the creation of all the sewing machines already made; and it can cause the creation of millions more, and will, whenever men set it in motion by desire and faith, and by acting in a Certain Way.

You can certainly have a sewing machine in your house; and it is just as certain that you can have any other thing or things which you want, and which you will use for the advancement of your own life and the lives of others.

You need not hesitate about asking largely; "it is your Father's pleasure to give you the kingdom," said Jesus.

Original Substance wants to live all that is possible in you, and wants you to have all that you can or will use for the living of the most abundant life.

"Do not forget that the Thinking Substance is through all, in all, communicating with all, and can influence all."
—Wallace Wattles

Chapter Six

How to Use the Will

What I'm going to teach you in this chapter is something that everybody should learn and hardly anybody knows: how to use the will. This is really how you change paradigms. Wattles says:

> When you know what to think and do, then you must use your will to compel yourself to think and do the right things. That is the legitimate use of the will in getting what you want—to use it in holding yourself to the right course. Use your will to keep yourself thinking and acting in the Certain Way.

Think of it this way—On one side is ignorance; on the other side is knowledge. There's a power flowing into your consciousness right now, and you can make anything you want out of it. You have the ability to think anything you want.

Say you're looking at your finances, and it's the fifteenth of the month. You've got to come up with $5,000 before the end of the month. You have no idea where this money is coming from, and you have virtually nothing in the bank. Now what should you be thinking, and what will you be thinking?

The power is flowing in. You can think anything you want. Now I'm going to tell you what most people do: they build a negative idea. They're working hard and saying, "I'm going to give everything I've got," but they're worrying, and they doubt their ability to do it. They get emotionally involved with an idea that sets up fear.

What has happened here? There's a power flowing in, and you can make anything you want out of it, but they use that power to create a negative concept. They're seeing what they *don't* want, and they get emotionally involved in it. That energy came in. They built an image and impressed that image on the screen of the mind. That's where the fear started.

Whatever is impressed must be expressed, so people express it as anxiety. If you're experiencing anxiety, there's the problem right there. But that's not where it stops, because the anxiety isn't expressed; we tend to suppress it. We bottle it up inside, and all hell breaks loose. We don't understand we're dealing with the delicate plastic instrument that is this body. When you suppress energy, it turns into depression: "It's a terrible world. What am I going to do?" Depression turns into the only thing it can—disease. The body starts breaking down. It's a slow form of suicide. We don't die; we kill ourselves.

Let's go back to the problem. There is nothing in the bank. We need $5,000. We have no idea how to get it. You ask, "How did I end up here? I don't know." You say the cause of the problem is that there's not enough money. That's not the cause at all. That's a symptom of the cause. The cause is ignorance.

You're thinking, aren't you? Damn right you are.

You can think anything you want. Why would you create anxiety in yourself? You're ignorant, but you know something? There's no allowance for ignorance. Someone may say they didn't know—tough, you still lose. A baby that walks out in front of a car will probably get killed, because the baby didn't know—too bad. A baby falls off of a balcony in a building seven stories high. You say, "My God! How could God let that happen?" God had nothing to do with that. The baby crawled off the balcony. The parent was the problem. They weren't looking after the baby. The baby didn't know, but there's no allowance for ignorance.

Do you see where I'm going? We're using the will here, but it's an improper use of the will. Don't tell me that people don't know how to use the will. They're using it. They are concentrating on the problem to the point of getting sick. "There's no money. What am I going to do?"

You could wake up. Let there be light. Blind faith is useless. Faith based on ignorance is wishing—useless nonsense going on in the mind. But faith based on understanding is the key to freedom.

We want to understand that this whole universe operates by law. We want to understand that everything on the physical plane came from the nonphysical. Lack and limitation are what we created. That's what we asked for, and that's what we got.

What's the opposite? We want to understand. We want to understand this law of opposites. We want to understand how to create. We want to understand we are creative beings that we have the ability to choose. But the only way to develop understanding is through study. There is no other way. You've got to study.

It sounds preposterous, but you could have an empty bank account, and if you have an image in your mind that $5,000 and more is going to be there, it'll be there. I don't know where it's coming from, but I know it's going to be there. Don't worry about it. Don't even think about not having it. Hold the image of the thing you want, keep that image, and impress it upon your subjective mind.

"Everything on the physical plane
came from the nonphysical. Lack and
limitation are what *we* created. That's what
we asked for, and that's what we got."
—Bob Proctor

You have faith. Faith is the ability to see the invisible and believe in the incredible, and that will enable you to receive what the masses say is impossible. Well-being, not anxiety, is the expression of faith. Well-being isn't suppressed; it's expressed. The expression accelerates, because you're at ease; you understand, and you create the good you want. It'll be there.

You have a choice. You can go the way of no control. That's how most people live. They're not in control of themselves at all. Or you can go the other way, and be in control. We want to be in control. I want to be in control of me.

We've got to understand the creative process: when we ask for what we want and expect it, it's going to manifest in our life just as surely as we're standing on the earth. It's so basic a truth, and yet so misunderstood. As we really start to understand this principle, everything in our life changes.

Since belief is all-important, it behooves you to guard your thoughts. As your beliefs will be shaped to a very great extent by the things you observe and think about, it's important to focus your attention on what you want. Focus is the key. Where focus goes, energy flows. You want to be in control of the flow.

Now here's the truth: most people live one way part of the time and the other way part of the time. Sometimes they act as if they're in control; other times, they act as if they're not. I'm suggesting that you don't have to live like that at all. I live like that periodically, but it's only for minutes. I would never stay there. The second I feel myself in that vibration, I stop it, because I know what I'm doing to me, and I go back to a positive state of mind.

"When we ask for what we want, and expect it, it's going to manifest in our life, as sure as we're standing on the earth."
—Bob Proctor

The Power of Gratitude

Chapter 7 of *The Science of Getting Rich* is devoted to gratitude. Wattles writes:

> The first step toward getting rich is to convey the idea of your wants to the Formless Substance.
>
> This is true, and you will see that in order to do so it becomes necessary to relate yourself to the Formless Intelligence in a harmonious way.
>
> To secure this harmonious relation is a matter of such primary and vital importance that I shall give some space to its discussion here, and give you instructions which, if you will follow them, will be certain to bring you into perfect unity of mind with God.

> The whole process of mental adjustment and atonement can be summed up in one word, *gratitude*.

He's talking about mental adjustment. Anytime we're frustrated, anytime we're getting down, anytime we're feeling in a low vibration, it's because of what's going on in our mind, so we have to adjust what's going on in our mind. We get in harmony with the good we desire and let go of anything that we're feeling angry or frustrated about.

This process also has to do with atonement. Atonement is to forgive, to release, to just let it go. We do that because we want to relate to the good that we desire. We want to be in harmony with it.

Wattles sets out three steps in this process: "First, you believe that there is one Intelligent Substance, from which all things proceed; second, you believe that this Substance gives you everything you desire; and third, you relate yourself to It by a feeling of deep and profound gratitude."

This is an emotional exercise, but also a profoundly spiritual one. We are relating ourselves to the source of all the good that comes to us, and we're doing it in a most reverent way, where we feel it in every cell of our being. We shift our vibration.

Wattles goes on to say:

Many people who order their lives rightly in all other ways are kept in poverty by their lack of gratitude. Having received one gift from God, they cut the wires which connect them with Him by failing to make acknowledgment.

It is easy to understand that the nearer we live to the source of wealth, the more wealth we shall receive; and it is easy also to understand that the soul that is always grateful lives in closer touch with God than the one which never looks to Him in thankful acknowledgment.

The more gratefully we fix our minds on the Supreme when good things come to us, the more good things we will receive, and the more rapidly they will come; and the reason simply is that the mental attitude of gratitude draws the mind into closer touch with the source from which the blessings come.

If it is a new thought to you that gratitude brings your whole mind into closer harmony with the creative energies of the universe, consider it well, and you will see that it is true. The good things you already have have come to you along the line of obedience to certain laws. Gratitude will lead your mind out along the ways by which things come; and it will keep you in close harmony with creative thought and prevent you from falling into competitive thought.

Gratitude focuses you on the good, not just for yourself, but for everyone you come in contact with. When you're on a creative plane, you want to leave everybody with the impression of increase. Your spirit is calling for increase. Your spiritual being wants fuller expression and expansion; so does the spirit of everybody else. When you understand that great truth, everything in your life truly changes, and the good starts to overflow in abundance.

We relate our self to the formless intelligence. We get in harmony with the good that we desire, and we shift our vibration to really feel the gratitude. The feeling is the key.

I'm going to give you a gratitude exercise, but I want to focus on a few things to set the foundation. Ask yourself these questions:

- Would you like you if you met you?
- Do you leave people with the impression of increase?
- Are you in a creative mindset?
- Do you share the beauty inside of you, or are you focused on negative things?

If you don't like your answers to any of those questions, that's OK. Don't feel bad. Just understand that you can change: you can set the objective of leaving everyone with the impression of increase. Carl Jung said, "I'm not what

---

Wallace Wattles' 3-step Gratitude Process:

1. Believe that there is one Intelligent Substance

2. Believe that this Substance gives you everything you desire

3. Relate yourself to It by a feeling of deep and profound gratitude.

---

has happened to me; I am what I choose to become." Don't get locked into what's happened. Don't think in reverse. Keep thinking forward. As you raise your level of awareness, you're recreating who you are.

It's not who you are that holds you back, it's who you think you're not. Who you are is something magnificent. Who you think you're not is just the paradigm that's blocking you from seeing the truth. Let that go. Let the old programming go. Respect yourself enough to walk away from anything that no longer serves you, helps you grow, or makes you happy.

Sit down and think about that. What do you have going on in your life—relationships, habits, work? If any of these no longer serves you, respect yourself enough to walk away from it. You owe it to yourself.

Peel off the masks of illusion, unshackle the chains of expectation, release the ingrained patterns, give up the stories of the past. Let go of the fear. It's never too late to be who you really are. Some of your paradigms are just limiting beliefs that you inherited; they're massive illusions that you can let go of.

What about the chains of expectation? How often do we do things because we think somebody else is expecting us to do it? Unshackle the chains of expectation, release those old patterns, and replace them with new patterns. Foremost, let go of the fear. It's never too late to be who you really are.

We want to lock in the idea that there is a marvelous inner world, and it's operating within you right now. The revelation of that world enables you to do and attain and achieve anything you desire within the bounds or limits of nature. Right now, there is a beautiful energy flowing to and through you, and it will enable you to do anything you desire. So let go of those limiting thoughts, let go of the limiting paradigm, and bring in more of beautiful energy to shape your life in a big beautiful way.

It's all here right now. We need to keep consciously connected. When we do, we're conscious of the source and creator of all power, and we realize and receive the many benefits that surround us. That's what gratitude is all about. It's keeping us consciously connected. Wattles said it beautifully: "The whole process of mental adjustment and atonement can be summed up in one word, gratitude."

> "The whole process of mental adjustment
> and atonement can be summed up
> in one word, *gratitude*."
> —Wallace Wattles

Anytime you find yourself upset, you've got a problem, or something's just not going your way, understand that it's going on in your mind. You've got to make a mental adjustment. When you sit down and you truly feel what you're grateful for, your problem goes away. There is real power in this exercise.

The gratitude exercise has three steps:

1. Think of ten things that you're grateful for, and write them down. Here is where you really want to exercise discipline to shift how you feel. Whatever you're writing down, really feel gratitude for it. Feel it in every cell of your being. Start with wherever is easy, so you can make the shift to that feeling. You're getting in touch with your spiritual essence, you're feeling extreme gratitude, and you're in harmony with the good.

   The items you write out can be things that are already in your physical world, but they can also be things that are not yet physically manifested in your world.

"So we've already got it on two planes.
Then by law, as long as we don't let go of it,
it must manifest in our physical world.
So we can be grateful now, before it's actually
here, because we know by law it's coming."
—Sandy Gallagher

This practice is so powerful because, as we know, we have three planes to our personality. We're spiritual beings, we're living in a physical body, and we have an intellect that taps us into our higher side. By practicing gratitude, we understand that we've got the good on the spiritual plane. We've got it on the intellectual plane, because we've decided that this is what we're going for, and we're using our imagination to lock into the good we desire. So we've already got it on two planes. Then by law, as long as we don't let go of it, it must manifest in our physical world. So we can be grateful now, before it's actually here, because we know by law it's coming.

This is a huge tool that I use to manifest everything that I want to manifest in my life. But again, the key here is really shifting your vibration. You want to feel this.

2. Be quiet for five minutes, and ask spirit for guidance for the day. Say, *I'm open to being guided, I'm listening, I'm tuning in. I want the guidance. I am going to follow the guidance and you're tuned in throughout the day to getting guidance from your higher self.*

   You may ask whether what you're getting is real guidance. If it's guidance, you know. It's like fishing. If you've ever gone fishing, you know when you get a fish on the hook; you know it's a fish. The same is true when you're getting guidance.

3. Send love to three people that are bothering you. If you can't think of anyone that's bothering you, that's great; don't conjure up somebody that you're going to make bother you. But also remember the question I mentioned above: would you like you if you met you? If the answer is no right now, send love to yourself.

   The idea here is to truly want for everybody else what you want for yourself, because you under-stand who you are, your connection to everybody else, and how everything operates in an orderly way, by law. You want to put good out there; you want to send love out there. This is not about the other person—not at all. It's about you and what vibration you are in. If you are angry at someone, if you're holding on to the idea that they wronged you and you don't let it go, you're blocking yourself from the good you desire. Your vibration is not in harmony with it.

You want to learn to send love, forgive, and let go. The key is to feel that feeling of love and let go of everything that doesn't serve you. Mental adjustment and atonement are the key.

This is a very powerful exercise. It's worth making a commitment to do it every single day. As you do it over and over and really get into it, everything is going to improve.

Proctor Gallagher Institute 3-step Gratitude Exercise:

1. Think of ten things that you are grateful for, and write them down.

2. Be quiet for five minutes and ask Spirit for guidance for the day.

3. Send love to three people that are bothering you and/or to yourself.

Chapter Eight

Further Use of the Will

"You cannot retain a true and clear vision of wealth if you are constantly turning your attention to opposing pictures, whether they be external or imaginary," writes Wattles in chapter 10 of his book.

This is a very important point. Let's see what we're up against. Your body has five electrical hookups—the senses—that pick information up from your outside world. Now 97 percent of the population is going in the wrong direction. Consequently, over 90 percent of the information that is banging into those sensory factors of yours is not that positive. Furthermore, a large amount of what's coming up from inside, from your paradigm, is not that positive either. So if you do not consciously and deliberately set up a system that you can follow to keep yourself locked into positive ideas, you're toast.

How do you do that? Through use of the will. Wattles continues:

> Do not tell of your past troubles of a financial nature, if you have had them; do not think of them at all. Do not tell of the poverty of your parents, or the hardships of your early life; to do any of these things is to mentally class yourself with the poor for the time being, and it will certainly check the movement of things in your direction.
>
> "Let the dead bury their dead," as Jesus said.
>
> Put poverty and all things that pertain to poverty completely behind you.

You must use your will to compel yourself to think and do the right things. If you don't use your will this way, you're going to get knocked off track. Your senses are bombarded from the outside world through radio, through television, through newspapers, through overhearing other people. It's everywhere you go.

As we've already seen, the whole universe is full of energy; it's all energy. You're going to attract to your physical instrument the energy that corresponds to its vibration. You've got an electronic switching station inside of your skull, and it's called a brain. When any of your senses are affected, a message goes screaming through a nerve passageway, activating a group of cells in your brain. The

---

You've got an electronic switching station inside of your skull, and it's called a brain.

---

message hits those cells, which then increase in amplitude of vibration. (They're always vibrating, because the law of vibration decrees that everything vibrates.) As a result, you move into that vibration.

I remember my grandmother. She was a dear little soul, and she had a big rocking chair that she used to sit in all the time. She would hear something bad on the radio, and she'd start crying about it. She would really get into it. At the time I used to think, "Grandma, why do you get upset about this? Why do you pay attention to this?" Grandma was really attracted to bad news; Grandma's paradigm kept listening to all that stuff. Now she was a dear little lady, and she would feel bad for these people, but she wasn't helping them sitting there crying.

I remember Doug Wead. He was a special assistant to the president of the United States. He wrote the foreword to my book *You Were Born Rich*. Doug Wead was a nice guy and a smart guy. But when he was in seminary, there were many problems going on over in Vietnam, and people were starving to death over there. Doug and three of his friends went on a food strike. They would go to the cafeteria at noon, get their trays, and sit at the table with empty plates and empty trays. This was his way of trying to get attention for these poor people who are starving. But he said one day he was sitting there, and it dawned on him: empty plates don't feed hungry people. He wasn't helping them.

Instead of feeling sorry and getting lost in some cause like that, the best thing you can do is help *you*. Be the best example you can be. When you have more than you need, you can start giving.

When you know what to think and do, you must use your will to compel yourself to think and do right things. That's the legitimate use of the will in getting what you want: to use it in holding yourself to the right course. Use your will to keep yourself thinking and acting, as Wattles puts it, "in a Certain Way." What's a "Certain Way"? By law.

It's so basic yet so misunderstood. You've got a beautiful thought in your mind, and you've got a will. Now you're going to get bombed from both sides, so you're going to have the negative too. You've got to keep the will to hold the beautiful idea.

Remember that we went through ignorance and knowledge. We said ignorance causes doubt and worry, which cause fear, which causes anxiety. We suppress the anxiety and that causes depression, which causes disease, which causes disintegration.

We don't have to do that. On the other side, we get involved in knowledge. How do you get there? By studying. What's the polar opposite of worry? Understanding.

As we've seen, the law of polarity is operating all the time. This law decrees that everything is both good and bad, but in truth it is neither; it just is. We have the good and the bad. There they are, and sitting right in the center, everything just is. Now, if we can remember this, it's going to be easy for us to utilize our will to keep ourselves on the right track.

Wattles writes, "Thought is the creative power, or the impelling force which causes the creative power to act." That creative power is within you. All the great leaders down through history have been in complete and unanimous agreement on this one point: we become what we think about.

Whatever you're thinking about, you're going to attract. Everything operates on frequencies. We call a certain substance *paper* because of the speed it's vibrating at. It used to be called *wood*, and prior to that it was called *earth*. The earth was attracted to a seed. The seed kept attracting energy and grew into a big tree. We cut the tree down and turned it into paper. It's still the same energy as it was when it was earth; it's just moving at a different speed.

Wattles continues, "Thinking in a Certain Way will bring riches to you, but you must not rely upon thought alone, paying no attention to personal action. That is the rock upon which many otherwise scientific metaphysical thinkers meet shipwreck—the failure to connect thought with personal action." If you believe you can just lie there and think what you desire is going to come to you, someone in a white coat will come and take you away. You can and must act on your ideas. Get out and make it happen. And if you're not doing things that produce results, you'd better take a look at your own thinking.

On the earth, there are many different vibrations: plants, rocks, metal. They're all energy, but they all vibrate at a different speed. As Earl Nightingale said, if I plant corn, a sweet food, and I plant nightshade, a deadly poison, right beside it, one will grow with the same abundance as another. The corn attracts different energy from the earth than the nightshade.

Take an acorn. Certain particles of energy are in harmony with the acorn. Because of this, these particles move towards the acorn from all sides. An attractive force is set up, and a certain energy will march to the acorn like an obedient soldier. In the acorn is a patterned plan that controls its vibratory rate. It attracts energy that's in harmony with it, and the energy becomes one with the acorn. The acorn starts to expand and burst through the earth, and it attracts from the earth and the atmosphere everything that's necessary to create an oak tree. The energy that created the oak tree was always here. It was attracted to the seed. The acorn is in the earth, the energy for the oak tree is in the universe, and the law of attraction has brought them together.

To paraphrase Earl Nightingale:
"If I plant corn, a sweet food, and
I plant nightshade, a deadly poison,
right beside it, one will grow with the
same abundance as the other."
Be sure you plant what you want
in the garden of your mind!

You operate exactly the same way. You have a patterned plan in you. It's the goal that you set. If you don't have a goal, then you've got a bunch of unrelated ideas, which will cause you to act randomly. But if you've got a clear picture, you're going to start to grow, and that picture is going to manifest in prosperity, satisfaction, happiness, growth, and victory. If your mind is in a confused state, you're going to go all over the place. This is so basic, yet so misunderstood.

What do we have to do? We have to make certain that our thinking is in harmony with the law. Think of your life as an hourglass. The sand in the top of the glass represents the future. The sand in the bottom of the glass represents the past. The past is gone. It's done, passé. You cannot change it. You don't know how much sand you have left in the top of the glass. There's only one thing that you know, and that's right here, right now. So don't worry about what you have been doing or what you're going to do in the future. What are you doing right now?

If you find your mind wandering, change it. Out of confusion comes order. Order is heaven's first law. When you get your mind into an orderly state, everything starts working beautifully. When do you start? You start right now.

Chapter Nine

Acting in the Certain Way

Many of today's most influential success ideas can be traced back to Napoleon Hill. When he was in his early twenties, he was working for a magazine as a young reporter. The magazine was going to do an article on wealthy people. Hill got the phenomenal job of interviewing the wealthiest man in the world at that time: Andrew Carnegie. This was in 1908. Hill got three hours with Carnegie.

Hill didn't know that Carnegie was looking for someone to carry out a task. Carnegie thought it was an absolute crime that people like himself, Henry Ford, Thomas Edison, and Harvey Firestone and others were going to their graves with all the knowledge they had locked up in their bones. All of them had come up from nothing.

Carnegie came over from Scotland as a very young boy to the East Coast of the United States; he started out with nothing but became the wealthiest man in the world.

As Hill was interviewing Carnegie, Carnegie thought, "This might be the guy I'm looking for." He was looking for someone that could organize all his knowledge and write down the laws of achievement so that anybody could learn what he knew.

At the end of the three-hour interview, Carnegie said to Hill, "This interview isn't ending; it's just beginning." He wanted Hill to come home with him. Hill was glad he asked, because Hill didn't have enough money to rent a hotel room.

Where was this kid's mind at? He didn't have enough money to rent a hotel room and he's going home with the wealthiest man in the world. That would be a bit of a trip in itself, but he spent three days with Carnegie. Carnegie kept asking him questions, and he kept asking Carnegie questions.

At the end of three days, Carnegie thought, "I think this is the guy." So he said, "Napoleon, you've got all the information. You know exactly how I've got here. I've spent three days sharing my entire philosophy with you. I want to ask you a question. Would you dedicate the rest of your life to an idea for which you will probably receive no material compensation for at least twenty years?"

At the time, Hill didn't know that Carnegie had a stop watch in his hand under the desk and was giving him sixty seconds to answer the question. Hill said, "Yes, I will" in twenty-nine seconds. (I've asked myself many times whether I would have said yes. I think I would have. If I'd spent three days with this guy, I would have a pretty good read on whether he was fair, and I don't think he'd ask me to do something that wasn't fair.)

Carnegie said, "I want you to organize and write the laws of achievement. I will give you letters of introduction to some of the most accomplished people in the world. You'll have no trouble getting in to see these people. I want you to spend time with them. I want you to ask them questions."

Carnegie continued, "Napoleon, long before you finish this, everything in you is going to want to quit. By the way, I'm not going to subsidize you. You're going to have to make your own way while you're doing this. But I'm going to give you something that you can use when you want to quit. I want you to say this to yourself: 'Andrew Carnegie, I'll not only equal your achievements in life, but I'm going to challenge you at the post and pass you at the grandstand.'"

Hill is broke, he's looking at the wealthiest man in the world, and he's making a commitment: "Andrew Carnegie, I'll not only equal your achievements in life, but I'm going to challenge you at the post and pass you at the grandstand."

At that point, Hill threw his pen on the floor and said, "Now you know darn well I'm not going to be able to do that."

But Carnegie had told him that if you plant an idea in your subconscious mind, it has to happen. He spent three days explaining all this, telling him about the subconscious mind and how it'll accept anything as real and then work at manifesting it.

Carnegie said, "I want you to make a commitment that you'll look in the mirror and repeat that every morning and every night for thirty days."

"I could do that," said Hill.

When he first started do this exercise, he thought he was being stupid. After the first time he read this statement, he said, "This is silly; this couldn't possibly happen." But he'd made a commitment, so he decided that he would stick with it and do it. After about fifteen days, he thought maybe that could happen. By the end of the month, he knew it would happen.

What I'm doing here is sharing the information that Hill gathered. I have studied this for a long time. Through the studies I've done, I've concluded that Carnegie made maybe fifty millionaires. Napoleon Hill may have made millions of millionaires.

Hill was given a vision, and he developed very powerful friends. His Mastermind group included Thomas Edison, Henry Ford, and Harvey Firestone. Ask yourself, who are your Mastermind partners? Whom am I mixing with? Whom am I really tapping into? I don't spend a lot of time with anybody that's not really making it happen, because their thinking will go into my subconscious mind.

Earl Nightingale, a broadcaster in Chicago, partnered up with Lloyd Conant. These two came together to sell a record called *The Strangest Secret*; they sold over a million copies all over the world. I was working with them when it was given the first Gold Record for a spoken record.

In 1963, I got ahold of *Success Unlimited*, a magazine that was put out by W. Clement Stone. (That was the forerunner to the *Success* magazine of today.) *Success Unlimited* was a little house organ that he used for his insurance companies. I saw an ad in the magazine that Nightingale-Conant was looking for consultants to work in their company. I thought, "I'm going to do that." By 1968, I was their vice president of sales.

Ask yourself:
Who are my Mastermind partners?
Who am I mixing with?
Who am I really tapping in to?

How did that happen? It happened because I kept listening to that record, and I kept listening to my mentor.

You get an idea in your consciousness. You hold that idea, and you plant it in your subconscious mind. That idea grows, becomes a desire, and ultimately changes the vibration you're in and the results that you're getting. That is really the whole philosophy that Napoleon Hill shared with us.

Most people are really extras in their own movie. Ask yourself, what do you really want?

Think of levels of vibration as frequencies. You think on frequencies, and these thoughts will produce the results that you're getting. Now you're never happy with the results you're getting, you always want more, so you say, "That's where I want to go." But you say, "I'm going to do that as soon as this changes. I'm going to do that as soon as I get the money. I'm going to do that as soon as the kids are out of school. I'm going to do that as soon as, as soon as . . ." and pretty soon, the decision dies. Shortly after that, the goal that you're seeking dies.

Why? Because your thoughts are down on a lower frequency, and your goal is up on a much higher frequency. Your mind and thoughts must operate on the same frequency as your goal. If your mind and thoughts are not operating on that same frequency, it is never going to happen. You've got to make a committed decision: "This is what I'm going to do." When you start talking about

---

To operate on a higher frequency, make a committed decision. Then think and act like the person you want to become.

---

the Science of Getting Rich, you don't screw around with ordinary decisions. It's got to be a committed decision: "This I will do."

Now I'm going to tell you what happens when you make a committed decision. You've got to think and act like the person you want to become. You'll notice you're not on that lower frequency anymore. You're up here on this higher frequency. When you're on that frequency and you start thinking those thoughts, the goal must manifest.

Want is the only prerequisite for making a decision: do you want to? This is what Hill started to understand after Carnegie spent three days explaining all this to him. You only have to want to. That's all you have to do.

But most people never learn how to make a decision. They're always going to do it at some point or another, and they fool around. Successful people make decisions very fast. When Carnegie asked Napoleon Hill to make a decision, he took only twenty-nine seconds.

But Hill had mixed something else with it: discipline.

If you're going to make it happen, you've got to discipline yourself. It doesn't matter what happens. You've got to discipline yourself to live by the law. This is what I have burned into my mind. That's what I want you to burn into your mind. Give yourself a command and then follow it.

You've got to have a goal. Write it on a card that you carry in your pocket. I've been doing this since October 21, 1961. I wrote on the card I was going to have $25,000 in my possession on New Year's Day, 1970. I gave myself almost ten years to do it. I really didn't believe it would happen, but I've learned if you write a lie on a card and you read it often enough, you're going to start to believe it. The great psychologist William James said back in 1900, "Believe, and your belief will create the fact." Is it going to be easy? No, it's not going to; it's going to be tough.

Sixty years is a long time, but I've never stopped studying this material. I study it every day. Here's what I've learned: you never change things by fighting existing reality. To change things, you've got to build a new model that makes the existing model obsolete. That's what studying these lessons is going to do for you. Get involved in this material. Share it with as many people as possible. There's no end to what you can do.

Let's turn to goals. A-type goals are those we already know how to reach; B-type goals involve doing what we think we can do. C-type goals are the ones that you really want to accomplish, but you don't know how. You don't *have* to know how. We've got to go higher, where it's all possible. It's closer than our breath. What stops us? Paradigms. The programming is stopping us from doing all we're capable of doing.

People sometimes ask, if spirit is perfect, how can we have lack in our soul? The truth is, you don't have any lack in your soul. The lack is in the paradigm, which is blocking the expression of the soul. You see, you don't have a soul; you *are* a soul. That's why there's perfection within you. That perfection is seeking expression within and through you. Why do you think we want to get things? The real, underlying reason is to express the perfection within us. No one knows what we're capable of doing.

An A-type goal is doing something you already know how to do. Years ago, a man came up to me and asked, "Hey, Bob, would you talk to me about my goal?"

"What's your goal?" I asked.

"I want to get a new car."

"OK. That's a good goal," I said. "What kind of car do you want?"

"A Pontiac."

"I've had Pontiacs," I said. "Those are nice cars. What are you driving now?"

"A Pontiac."

"How long have you had it?"

"Four years."

"How old is it?"

"Four years."

"So what you've really told me is that you bought a new Pontiac four years ago."

"Yeah."

"You've known for four years how to get a Pontiac, so that's not a good goal. It doesn't mean you shouldn't get the Pontiac, but it would not constitute a goal. A goal is something that you don't know how to get."

When most people make the transition and go beyond what they already know how to get, they go after what they think they can do. So they set the goal this way: "If I get this money, if she paid me what she owed me, if he gives me what I need, and if they do this and if they do that, and if all these things fall in place, then I could reach the goal."

There's no inspiration in that. You've got to get up where the air is a little thin; you've got to fantasize. But as little kids, we were taught not to do that. If we go from here to there but we don't get the support and it doesn't work out, we come back to the starting point. Most people just stay there. Dare what you want to go after. Bet on yourself. You're the surest thing in the world.

There are three stages of creation: fantasy, theory, and fact. Where do you start? You're thinking of what you want, you start to fantasize, and you get a beautiful picture in your mind.

You're not going to get what you want just by fantasizing. You've got to take the next stage. You've got to take your fantasy and turn it into a theory.

When you use your reasoning mind, you start to think about what you want, but you've got to pass a test before you can turn the theory into a goal. You have to ask, "Am I able to do this?" Since you've got infinite potential, of course you can do it.

Then you have to ask, "Am I willing? Am I willing to do what has to be done?" You've got to be willing to do whatever it takes, which is what Hill did.

After reading and listening to audios and my mentor, I made up my mind that I would do it.

In Chicago in 1973, I was still at Nightingale-Conant Corporation, and I left only for one reason. I was selling records and cassettes; I was watching people buy them, but they weren't using them. I went to Lloyd Conant and I said, "Lloyd, we should give them the cassettes. Sell seminars, and give them the recording."

"No, no," he said. "We're going to leave the seminar business to Dale Carnegie; we're going to stay in the tape business."

I knew then it was time for me to leave.

I had gone there to get an education. I got an education. I was sitting at home. I was sitting in a little room in a house in Glenview, Illinois. I took my pen and wrote,

"I'm going to build a company that operates all over the world."

I said, "Yes, I'm able. Yes, I'm willing," and bingo! That became my goal. And I turned my goal into reality. Now we have had events where we stream into every country. And we have consultants in ninety-two countries.

When you accomplish one goal, you're in the position to build bigger and better fantasies. That's the creative process.

You've got to stretch, baby. You've really got to stretch. You have to go after a C goal. You don't have to know what to do to get there, but you have to know that you're going to do it. It's that simple.

Napoleon Hill said, "There's a difference between wishing for a thing and being ready to receive it. No one's

---

3 Types of Goals:

1. A-Goals: Those goals you already know how to accomplish.

2. B-Goals: Those goals you think, but are not absolutely certain, you can accomplish.

3. C-Goals: Those goals that you really want to accomplish, but you don't know how. This where high achievers put their focus. They know they can find out how—this challenge doesn't stop them.

ready for a thing until they believe they can acquire it. The state of mind must be belief, not mere hope or wish." Most people hope and wish things will happen; that isn't going to work. It never has worked. You've got to believe it. When you believe it, everything starts to happen.

Napoleon Hill also said, "No more effort is required in order to aim high in life, to demand abundance and prosperity, than is required to accept misery and poverty."

Now I'm going to show you how and why all this works. You are a mass of energy. If we took a picture of you with a Kirlian camera, the energy leaving your body would be so powerful that it would penetrate the camera and the film, and we could actually photograph the energy leaving your body. You are one powerful soul.

A frequency, as we saw earlier, is a level of vibration. There's an infinite number of frequencies. Every one is connected to the one above and one below. There's no line of demarcation. That means we've got to go beyond our five senses. We've got to go into the fourth dimension, a higher dimension of thought, which is beyond the body.

Einstein said the intuitive mind is a sacred gift; the rational mind is a faithful servant. We have created a society that honors the servant and has forgotten the gift. We've got all these higher faculties—perception, memory, imagination, reason, intuition, and will. They're the tools that help us connect with the unseen.

If you take an honest look at your life, you'll see how you've gotten to where you are. Everything you have is nothing but an expression of your own level of awareness. Remember when you left school and got your first job. Remember when you met your spouse, went on your first flight, and so on.

Take a look at where you are right now in your life. I'm going to tell you something: you're not going to be satisfied with where you are. You want to go further. Why? Because you're a spiritual being, and spirit is always for expansion and fuller expression, but we don't have to know how to get to where we want to go.

When we were little kids, we would say, "Mommy, Daddy, I want this!"

They would say, "How are you going to do that?"

We didn't know how, and so we just let it go; we let it fade.

We're living on an AM frequency, and we're trying to get FM music. It won't happen. If you phone your brother, you're not going to get your mother. You've got to get on the frequency of the good that you desire. The moment your belief matches with a state, the moment you believe you can do what you long to do, you fuse with it. You're emotionally, intellectually, and physically involved, your whole being is vibrating on that frequency, and you have an inner knowing that you can do it. You don't know how, but you know you can.

This new conscious state of awareness becomes your home. You've got to live there. Don't leave it; stay there. That's your home, and that's your workshop. If you're observant, you're going to see your outer reality shape itself upon the model of your imagination.

When you move on to a higher frequency, you're going to be communicating with a world that's totally foreign to and beyond the reach of your five senses. You're not going to see how to do it. It doesn't matter. Trust me. Believe what these authors are telling us. Believe what I'm telling you. Quit talking to the guy next door or your brother-in-law.

Steve Jobs of Apple said that you cannot connect the dots going forward; you can only connect them looking backwards. When you get to where you want to be and look back, you see how it all happened, but you don't know how it *will* happen. You've got to trust, so you start moving, and isn't it strange? The pieces all fall in place.

You've got to control the flow of thought energy. You've got to let it flow freely to and through you. To

---

"When you move on to a higher frequency, you're going to be communicating with a world that's totally foreign to and beyond the reach of your five senses."
—Bob Proctor

---

move to a considerably higher frequency of thought, first you have to consent. It's got to be your decision. Then you have to adapt to the ideas and feelings represented by the new frequency. Nobody else can help you.

It's not always going to be easy. At the suggestion of a move, your paradigm is instantly going to put up a real battle; it'll continually fight you. You've got to take conscious control over your paradigm and replace it. If you don't, you'll stay where you are. You can get help, but ultimately you're the one who has to do it.

When I asked, what do you really want? an idea may have come to your mind, but possibly you shut it down: "I couldn't do that. We couldn't afford that. I don't know the right people." You're going to hit a brick wall, but it isn't brick, and it's not a wall. It's imaginary.

If you latch onto your goal, you're going to have to go through four stages of growth, which lead to understanding and freedom.

The first stage is *bondage*. Basically, you've got your X-type conditioning—the conditioning you've had for a long time. Consequently, you're engaging in X-type behavior, taking X-type actions, entertaining X-type thoughts and voilà! You're getting X-type results.

Most people are in bondage. In fact you could look at some people that are, in your mind, extremely successful, but if they're doing the same thing over and over and thinking the same way over and over, they're in bondage.

> "If you latch onto your goal, you're going
> to have to go through four stages of growth,
> which lead to understanding and freedom."
> —Sandy Gallagher

To continue to grow, you've got to move out of the stage of bondage and move into the stage of *reason*, where you start to entertain a Y idea. A Y idea is a big idea that's different than the way you're conditioned to think. You start to entertain this idea, but only in your conscious mind. You're still taking X-type actions and getting X-type results. Even fewer people get past that stage—a tiny percentage of the population get past that stage.

When you get past that stage, you go into the stage of the *terror barrier*. The final stage, which ever few reach, involves going through the terror barrier into the stage of *freedom*. This is what we are all searching for.

Let's go look at this in a little more detail. Say that you're really making it happen in your life, but it's all in harmony with your X-type conditioning. Meta physical author Thomas Troward calls it a circle of ignorance:

We habitually look at the mechanical side of things by preference to any other. Everything is done mechanically, from the carving on a piece of furniture to the arrangement of the social system. It is the mechanism that must be considered first, and the spirit has to be fitted to the mechanical exigencies. We enter into the mechanism of it instead of into the Spirit of it, and so limit the Spirit and refuse to let it have its own way; and then, as a consequence, we get entirely mechanical action, and complete our circle of ignorance by supposing that this is the only sort of action there is.

Say you're in this stage of bondage, and you've got X-type conditioning in your subconscious mind. That's your paradigm, the emotional part of your personality. In your conscious mind, you're going to only be entertaining X-type ideas. Countless ideas are floating into your mind, but you filter out all the ones that aren't in harmony with your X-type conditioning. You've got to get past this stage and start entertaining new ideas— ideas that your level of awareness hasn't opened up to before.

To get past that stage and change the results in your life, you say, "I am going to expand my consciousness," and you go on to stage two: reason. You've got a big beautiful idea that you love. You think about it and start playing around with it in your conscious mind. You start to tap into your intellectual faculties, your imagination. You're thinking, "Wow! I could do this."

At this point, you impress the idea on your subconscious mind, get emotionally involved with it, and see yourself accomplishing it. Then boom! You hit that terror barrier. Worry, doubt, fear, and anxiety hit you. It's as if your central nervous system is short-circuiting, and all you want to do is run back to the comfort zone.

Most people get stuck here. If they get this far, they get up to the terror barrier and go flying back to safety. They do this over and over, and eventually start thinking, "It's not so bad here."

Why is this such a scary place to come to? Because the old and new conditioning are like oil and water. They do not mix, creating a chaotic vibration. You might experience a headache or feel nauseous, or just feel chaos and anxiety.

That's natural. That is coming up against the terror barrier. That's the paradigm battling with the dream, and you cannot let the paradigm win. Unfortunately, as people fail to go through the terror barrier and keep getting knocked back to safety, they're kicked down on the ladder of self-esteem. But you've got to go to the next stage. As Joseph Campbell puts it, "The cave you fear to enter holds the treasure you seek."

"That's the paradigm battling with the dream, and you cannot let the paradigm win."
—Sandy Gallagher

When you face the fear, you automatically experience the growth that you're seeking. It's a spiritual part of you that is seeking that growth. This is something you really want. This is inspiring you; it's your heart's desire. You want to go through to the next stage, so that this can be yours. That is freedom.

At this point, you've impressed your idea on the subconscious mind. You've got to keep impressing it over and over, because it's still mixed energy—the old and new paradigms. You keep mixing them until finally you've changed your paradigm.

Guess what you have to do at that point? Set a bigger and a better goal. But you've tasted freedom, and you love it, because it's the essence of who we are. Spirit wants that freedom and expansion.

I've already mentioned mental hurry. Hurry is fear and consequently destructive. You may experience it at this terror stage. You're standing still, but you feel as if your legs are running in place, and you just want to get out of there. Are you going to go running back, or are you going to go through the terror barrier? Jump: you'll develop wings along the way!

As you go through the terror barrier, you'll be so proud and grateful that you did. Sometimes you get an email or have a conversation that confirms you are on your course, and it will make you feel so good. If you get a communication like this, you might want to print it out, laminate it, and keep it.

Now ask yourself, what stage do you really think you're at right now? You may have gone through this process before and had some big changes in your life. Then maybe you quit growing, quit studying, quit working on yourself. What stage are you right now? That's the only thing that's really important.

It's about being willing to change your thinking and go against the strong current. That is key. Just do everything you can every day. You may not see evidence that it's working, but it is working if you're holding the idea, emotionally involving yourself in it, impressing on your subconscious mind, and acting in harmony with it. Do everything you can every day. Be willing to change your thinking and go against the flow. Go through that terror barrier. It doesn't happen by accident, but it's a beautiful thing when you make it happen. Your spirit wants expansion and fuller expression.

The 4 Stages of Growth when pursuing a goal:

Stage One: Bondage

Stage Two: Reason

Stage Three: The Terror Barrier

Stage Four: Freedom

Chapter Ten

The Impression of Increase

Everybody wants increase. Let's look at what Wallace Wattles says about it:

> Increase is what all men and all women are seeking; it is the urge of the Formless Intelligence within them, seeking fuller expression.
>
> The desire for increase is inherent in all nature; it is the fundamental impulse of the universe. All human activities are based on the desire for increase. People are seeking more food, more clothes, better shelter, more luxury, more beauty, more knowledge, more pleasure—increase in something, more life.
>
> Every living thing is under this necessity for continuous advancement; where increase of life ceases, dissolution and death set in at once.

Man instinctively knows this, and hence he is forever seeking more.

Yet many of us are raised to think that we shouldn't want more.

Our conditioning may go back generations and generations: "You don't need all that; be happy; be satisfied with what you've got."

It's not crazy to want more. If we know who we are and we understand our spiritual nature, of course we want more. We want increase. We're God's highest form of creation, so we want to create, and that means increase.

When we realize that everybody wants this, we want to know how to give it to others. Wattles says, "You can convey this impression by holding the unshakable faith that you, yourself, are in the Way of Increase; and by letting this faith inspire, fill, and permeate every action."

It's not always easy to hold this state and let it permeate every action that you take. Sometimes you have problems, you start to think of lack and limitation, you're feeling stressed, you're resisting the problems, and you're putting that energy out. But if we shift our perception, we realize that these problems are a way for us to grow and raise our conscious awareness. And if we raise our conscious awareness, we have more that we can give. As Wattles writes, we "must so hold the Advancing Thought

"We're God's highest form of creation, so we want to create, and that means increase."
—Sandy Gallagher

that the impression of Increase will be communicated" to all with whom we come in contact. It's critical to keep growing and expanding our awareness and entertaining new ideas. Then we continually have more to convey to others.

Are you leaving people with "the Impression of Increase"? Because everything you are thinking—not just what you're saying—is being conveyed to the people around you. And if their subconscious mind is wide open, it goes right in. If you're feeling insecure, if you're feeling angry, frustrated, you're feeling lack or limitation, you're conveying that to others, and they're going to feel the way you're feeling.

What are you putting out? Every thought you have affects others, so don't be that person that's thinking negatively, complaining, or nitpicking. Whatever you're sending out is coming right back at you; keep that in mind. See abundance, see opportunity; really feel it. See increase and give that to everyone you come in contact with. Everybody wants freedom, expansion, and expression, because we want more life. When you can give this to others, they'll love you for it.

"The most powerful paradigm-shifting
tool on earth is the human soul on fire."
—Sandy Gallagher

The most powerful paradigm-shifting tool on earth is the human soul on fire. Earl Nightingale talked about the surging dream, a dynamic thing, invisible to all the world except to the person who holds it. It drives you, you're on fire, and you're growing. You're giving more to others just by virtue of raising your consciousness; you are increasing your ability to leave everyone with the impression of increase.

The results you're getting in life are an expression of your level of awareness. If you watch people, you can see where they are. You can see what their level of awareness is. When you get frustrated with somebody else, remember that their awareness is on one level, while your level of awareness is on another. They don't understand where you are or how you got there, but you can see where they are and how they got there. Don't criticize them; don't get frustrated with them; just understand that they don't know.

The same is true with you. When you're with someone on a higher level of awareness, you're not necessarily going to understand what they're talking about. Open your mind and just say, "OK, I'm going to keep growing. I'm going to get better results, because I'm going to continue to expand my level of awareness."

"The answer to prayer is not according to the faith that you have while you're talking," says Wattles, "but according to your faith while you are working." Let everything you do demonstrate your faith.

You see people that are struggling, even though very educated, with any number of degrees. Lots of things in their lives would indicate that they would be doing really well, yet you see them struggling and stuck. Then you see other people that may not have many of the things that we would think are needed to succeed, yet they're incredibly successful.

Why? It's because of what's going on inside our mind. So we've got to always be aware of what's going on inside our mind, and we've got to be in control of it. It's a mind game, and we've got to be in charge of that game.

Effective goals inspire you to move to higher levels of awareness, wealth, happiness, and peace of mind. There's a basic law of life, which states that everything in the universe is either in a state of creation or disintegration. You can't stay in one place. You're either going forward or you're going backward, so you'd better make sure you're going forward. Absolutely nothing stands still. Your life is either moving in one direction or it's moving in the other, and it's your choice. Which way are you going to go? Are you creating? Are you moving up in your level of awareness or are you going down, disintegrating, going backwards? It's your choice.

There's a battle going on inside of us, like the Battle of Armageddon: you've got the higher side of your personality, which is urging you to create and to express more of yourself, and you have the other side, which is saying, "Wait, stay down here." It's trying to pull you down.

You've got to win that battle. Make sure you're always moving towards the higher side.

Wattles says, "The normal desire for increased wealth is not an evil or reprehensible thing. It is simply the desire for more abundant life. And because it is the deepest instinct of their natures, all people are attracted to an individual who can give them more of the means of life."

Your higher side's urging you to create, to grow. Your old paradigm wants to hold you down, so you have to keep moving forward to new levels of awareness. Remember, you don't have to know how you're going to do it. You

"Your higher side is urging you to create, to grow. Your old paradigm wants to hold you down, so you have to keep moving forward to new levels of awareness."
—Sandy Gallagher

just have to know you will. As you keep moving forward and taking action, doing what you can each day, you're going to be creating new conditions and circumstances. Your environment will change, and as you adapt to these changes, you can see the next step.

You then can move to the next level, to a higher level of life. The way is revealed as you keep moving higher, and as you keep moving up, the battle keeps going on. But you know what? It gets easier to win that battle and keep moving higher.

There's a great story about Jimmy Carter and Admiral Hyman Rickover, which Carter tells in his book *Why Not the Best?* Carter was a graduate of the Naval Academy, and he wanted to get into the nuclear submarine program. Because that was intense work, you had to go through a very challenging interview process, including a two-hour interview with Admiral Hyman Rickover. Admiral Rickover was the longest-serving person in the armed services of the United States. He served for over sixty years in the Navy, and he's known as the father of the nuclear program.

Carter knew that he was going to have a two-hour interview with Rickover, and everyone told him this was going to be really intense. There was a whole series of topics, and he was able to choose those he wanted to be interviewed on. He picked his favorites, including music and ballistics.

During the interview, Rickover would ask Carter a series of questions, each of which got progressively harder. Carter said that Rickover wouldn't blink or smile; he would just look right at him and ask the question. Carter got to the point where he was in a wet sweat, because he quickly realized that he didn't know as much as he needed to know about any topic; Rickover knew so much more than him.

Rickover got to the topic of the Naval Academy and asked Carter, "How did you do in the Naval Academy?" Carter was relieved to get this question, because he did well in the Naval Academy. He puffed up and said, "I was fifty-ninth out of 820."

Carter was waiting for Rickover to congratulate him, but Rickover just looked at him and turned his back. He asked one more question: "Did you do your best?"

Carter thought for a minute and started to say yes. But he knew this was Rickover, so he said, "No, I probably didn't do my best in every area."

Rickover turned around for a second and said, "Why not?" He turned his back to Carter again and never turned again to him.

Carter sat there for a moment; then he walked out of the room, feeling horrible. But it turned out well for him, because that question drove him to do his best always. And of course he ended up in the White House.

"You are getting continuous increase for yourself," wrote Wattles, "and you are giving it to all with whom you deal. You are a creative center, from which increase is given off to all."

You are a channel through which God works, and God wants you to do your best. You're a channel, and you have this power. As you continually become more aware of this truth, you can convey more increase. That's what Wattles is talking about. That's what Rickover was talking about: doing your best. Author Robert Russell puts it well: "There's no secret to greatness. It's just doing small things in a great way every single day."

As we bring this book to a close, let us remind you of the main thing: you've got one life; you get one bite of the apple. If you're not living the way you really want to live, you'd better change it.

"There's no secret to greatness. It's just doing small things in a great way every single day."
—Robert Russell

About the Authors

To millions of people across the globe, the name Bob Proctor is synonymous with success. Long before his role in the movie *The Secret* sent him into superstardom, he was already a legendary figure in the personal development industry. His insights, inspiration, ideas, systems, and strategies provided the sparks that ignited career transformations, personal epiphanies, inner awakenings, and the creation of million-dollar fortunes all around the world.

Bob was the heir to the modern science of success legacy that began with the financier and philanthropist Andrew Carnegie. Carnegie's great challenge to the young reporter Napoleon Hill to discern a formula for success fueled Hill's creation of the renowned book *Think and Grow Rich*. Upon discovering this book at the age of twenty-six, Bob's life changed instantly, leading him on his own quest for the secrets of success. That quest led him to Earl Nightingale, the famed "Dean of Personal Development," who soon became Bob's colleague and mentor. Bob continued to build upon and spread the remarkable teachings of these three giants until his death in February of 2022.

Bob Proctor worked with business entities and individuals worldwide as a speaker, author, consultant, coach, and mentor. He instilled the mental foundations of success, the motivation to achieve, and the actionable strategies that empower people to grow, improve, and thrive in this ever-changing world.

Sandy Gallagher was an esteemed attorney with a successful career in banking law. She regularly handled billions of dollars in mergers and acquisitions, IPOs, and other big-ticket transactions, and was an advisor to boards and top executives of Fortune 500 firms.

Then an encounter with personal development authority Bob Proctor set Sandy on a new path that would change her life. Through Bob's teachings, Sandy finally understood the "why" behind all of her success and she knew then that her next mission in life was to teach others how to do what she had done. She became determined to join forces with Bob in order to fulfill that mission.

Sandy ended up collaborating with Bob on a program called *Thinking Into Results*, which is the most powerful corporate transformational program of its kind.

Through the Proctor Gallagher Institute, Sandy Gallagher and the team Bob mentored continue to teach the principles, strategies, and fundamentals that help people and organizations create the results they want.

9 781722 505769